Mental-pause

...and Other Midlife Laughs

Laura Jensen Walker

Foreword by Martha Bolton

 Fleming H. Revell

A Division of Baker Book House Co
Grand Rapids, Michigan 49516

Published by Fleming H. Revell
a division of Baker Book House Company
P.O. Box 6287, Grand Rapids, MI 49516-6287

Printed in the United States of America

Library of Congress Cataloging-in-Publication Data

Walker, Laura Jensen.
    Mentalpause . . . and other midlife laughs / Laura Jensen Walker.
       p.   cm.
    ISBN 0-8007-5759-9
    1. Menopause—Humor. 2. Middle aged women—Health and hygiene—Humor.

RG186.W28 2001
618.1′75′00207—dc21   2001019321

For current information about all releases from Baker Book House, visit our web site:
                http://www.bakerbooks.com

Mental-pause

...and Other Midlife Laughs

For Adelaide, beloved family matriarch, who handles aging—and everything else—with grace, beauty, laughter, kindness, and much love. I want to be like you when I grow up.

And for Katie, my funny mentalpause friend, who never forgets to laugh in all the right places.

Contents

Foreword

by Martha Bolton

Hot flashes, night sweats, mood swings, uncontrollable crying for no apparent reason—sound like fun? Of course not. Nobody looks forward to dealing with the symptoms of menopause, but just like you have to tell yourself in the waiting room of your dentist's office—get ready, your turn is coming.

Middle age seems to hit men differently. They dye their hair, shop in the youth section of department stores, buy a brand-new red sports car, change the settings on their radio from talk to pop, and start conversing in a sort of middle-age hip language that few understand, saying things like, "I'm goin' down to the shuffleboard court to hang with my homies" or "Yo, where's my corn pads?" It's sad, but I still say they have it easier than women. Men don't have to worry that their next hot flash is going to set their clothes ablaze, or that someday they're going to drown in their sleep during a *Perfect Storm*–sized night sweat. Their moods don't swing between Betty Crocker and Lizzie Borden, and they don't break down crying watching Federal Express commercials. Even if a middle-aged man starts dressing like John Travolta in his disco days, while that's serious, it's still not nearly as bad as what women have to go through.

So how do women cope? How else? By laughing about it! Maybe not about all of it, but certainly those areas where we can laugh. After all, if we have to hit middle age (and so far there's no detour around it), then why shouldn't we have as much fun with it as possible?

That's what Laura has done within the pages of her new book. With her usual wit and wisdom, she's reminded us that there is a funny side to getting older, just like there's a funny side to every stage of our life. We tend to forget that. It's there. It's always there. But it's up to us to look for it. When you think about the diligence with which we look for those new wrinkles or grey hairs, looking for a little humor in these over-forty years seems a lot more profitable.

Laura has also learned that life is precious. We have to savor every moment and make it last. Yesterday is gone. We have little control over tomorrow. All we have is today! It's up to us not to waste it. And in my opinion, a hearty laugh is proof that we haven't wasted the day.

So read, laugh, and enjoy! And remember not to let those ol' age spots get to you. They're going to come anyway. You can't fight it. So just do what I do. Wait 'til they connect, then pass them as off as a tan!

Martha Bolton
Staff writer for Bob Hope
Author of over 40 books, including *I Love You . . . Still* and *Didn't My Skin Used to Fit?*

Acknowledgments

When you write a book on midlife and all the attendant "m's" that go along with it, menopause, mood swings, memory loss . . . it's kind of hard to remember everyone to thank, but I'll give it the good old middle-aged try.

First, my heartfelt thanks to everyone who so graciously shared their funny midlife stories with me: Charlotte Adelsperger, Jerry Bauman, Judi Braddy, Kathy Christensen, Peggy Clark, Jan Coleman, Barb Colwell, Lisa Jensen Cook, Debbie Cullifer, Susie Dayton, Merrie Douglas, Marjean DuPree, Eve Dorf, Lonnie Hull DuPont, Carolyn Elder, Bettie Eichenberg, Cathy Evans, Karen Graham, Karen Grant, Jean Griswold, Sharon and Jim Hetland, Maria Hunt, Kat Hunter, Sheri Jameson, Ruth Kenney, Sue Lenart, Pat and Ken McLatchey, Bonnie Mouw, Diana Nelson, Joyce Pope, Char Roushia, Beverly Pierce Stroebel, Jill Vanderbrug, June Varnum, Carolyn White, Charles and Mary West, Katie Young, and Trisha. Although every anecdote didn't make it into the book, I appreciate all your contributions.

Special thanks to Karen Grant who let me spend a delightful morning interviewing her and who gave me gobs and gobs of great menopausal stuff to use.

Ditto to my longtime friends Pat and Ken McLatchey and to my sweet sister-in-law Sheri Jameson and her friends, Merrie and M. J.

A very special thanks to my funny writer friend Jan Coleman who promptly responded to my frantic last-minute phone call and helped me brainstorm the Middle-Age Top 40 chapter when my brain was in severe mentalpause overload. Jan, you're a lifesaver!

Continued thanks to my talented poet friend Katie Young for her invaluable humorous input and . . . actually, this time I'm not going to list all my thanks to you, Katie. After all, I dedicated the book to you—what more could you want? Love ya, DaVinci.

Deepest gratitude and love to my mom and my sister (thanks for the great dropped derriere anecdote, Lee) whom I'm proud to call not only relatives but friends.

To my computer whiz nephew Josh who rode gallantly to the rescue when my laptop crashed—right on deadline: Gigabyte thanks. Or is it megabyte? Whatever. Josh, you're my computer hero.

Love and thanks to my best friend Lana who's not quite at that middle-age point yet so couldn't contribute any up close and personal stories of her own, but who was as supportive as always of my writing. Besides, your midlife day will come, babe. (Those bifocals I was surprised to see you pull out at Christmas are only the beginning. . . .)

Warm gratitude, as always, to my absolutely fabulous editor and friend, Lonnie Hull DuPont, who makes the whole creative experience such a pleasure—and so much fun! We truly were separated at birth. Thanks for your expert editorial gifts and for always going to bat for me—it's a privilege working with you. (And many thanks for singing the menopausal mustache song at sales conference.)

To Marketing Wonder Woman Twila Bennett . . . what can I say? You're the top, girlfriend. Have they bought you your own red cape yet? With you in my corner, I know that I'm never "On My Own." Remember, we'll always have New York.

To the fabulous Baker Boys, Don Stephenson, Dave Lewis, Ruth Waybrant, Sheila Ingram, Sharon Van Houten, and everyone else in my wonderful Revell family—including the great sales reps—thank you so much for going above and beyond in all that you do. You guys are the best, and I love working with you. (And thanks for yet another great cover, Cheryl!)

To my agent, Chip MacGregor, whose off-the-wall sense of humor and keen editorial instinct zeroed in on my casual mention of mid-life and menopause as a possible book idea someday. "No, Laura! You must do this book NOW!" Thanks, Chip, and may you be the first man to ever experience the joy of hot flashes.

To my beloved Michael: Thanks for another great title, honey, and for putting up with me through all the hot flashes, mentalpause moments, and another crash deadline. But thanks most of all for loving me, age spots, sagging flesh, and all. You're my Don Quixote. And I'll always be your Dulcinea.

And last, but not least, thank you, God, for middle age. I'm grateful to be here to go through it.

Introduction

There is a time for everything, and a season
for every activity under heaven.
ECCLESIASTES 3:1

When my friends and family learned I was writing a book on middle age and menopause, they were more than a little surprised. "Laura, you're not even forty-five!" they said.

True.

But thanks to chemotherapy in my midthirties for breast cancer, I started on my menopausal trip a little earlier than normal.

I never was that big on "normal" anyway.

But let me say straight up how happy I am to be making this midlife trip—even on those days when I've misplaced the map, forgotten the car keys, and had an unexpected monthly visitor (whom I'd hoped to never ever see again) return.

Sure beats the alternative.

Okay, so I don't have the hard body of a twenty-year-old anymore. (Didn't even at twenty.)

And I'm in bed by 10:00 most nights.

And the memory's starting to go.

And . . . what was that other thing I was going to say?

From middle-age spread to gray hair and no-longer-perky breasts, it's a menopausal fact of life that, after forty, the body simply starts to go.

Along with everything else.

In fact, right this very moment as I'm finishing this book in the last days of the year 2000, I just read an article on the Internet that confirms this.

Research presented to the British Psychological Society in London showed that our reaction times, concentration span and powers of memory start to decline markedly from the age of 40 to 45 years onwards.

MIKE COLLETT-WHITE, REUTERS, DECEMBER 20, 2000

Never thought I'd be on the same page—mental or otherwise—with an English psychological society.

Lah-di-dah.

But the following e-mail on aging that a friend forwarded to me (no source given) says it more in my kind of language:

Midlife is when your memory really starts to go—the only thing you still retain is water. Midlife is when you want to grab every firm young lovely in a tube top and scream, "Listen, honey, even the Roman Empire fell, and those things will too!"

As a breast cancer survivor, I'm more conscious of "those things" than most.

But I'm also crystal clear on the fact that—saggy, perky, or otherwise—they don't define me as a woman.

Nor does menopause.

For many women, The Change is not a pleasant experience. In fact, for some, it's downright dreadful. We're all different, and our bodies respond differently to these physiological changes.

But having gone through breast cancer and chemo, for me menopause is a walk in the park—so far.

A walk I'm very grateful to be making.

Granted, I'm a little young to be making the m&m (midlife and menopause) journey, which is why I've interviewed other women who have traveled the road before me.

Whatever path I wind up following, I plan to pack plenty of humor for the trip. In the words of Ed Howe: "If you don't learn to laugh at trouble, you won't have anything to laugh at when you grow old."

My body and mind may be sagging a little these days, but my spirit's firm and soaring.

The creation itself will be liberated from its bondage to decay and brought into the glorious freedom of the children of God.

ROMANS 8:21

one

Mentalpause

They say the mind is the first thing to go . . .
at least, I *think* that's what they say.

My memory is so bad that many times
I forget my own name.

CERVANTES

I'm forty-two and having hot flashes.

What's up with *that*? I mean, forty-two??? C'mon! I thought that wasn't supposed to happen until I was around *sixty*-two.

My husband, Michael, who is three and a half years younger than I am, likes to joke, "I'm not even forty yet, and my wife is going through menopause."

But it's not just menopause, it's *mental*pause.

My memory is gone.

I'll be in the middle of an important conversation, start to begin a new sentence, and poof, it's vanished. Lost forever in the Bermuda triangle of mentalpause.

Or I can't remember names of common things around the house.

Like door.

Sink.

Husband.

I'll be explaining something to whatshisname, perhaps discussing a project that needs to get done, and the name of the item I'm discussing simply eludes me (although the project doesn't, much to my husband's dismay).

Finally, I point at the offending object in frustration and say, "Whatever that thing is called. You *know* what I'm talking about!"

Pointing has become my latest aerobic activity, and *whatchamacallit* is my noun of choice these days.

It's not as if my memory's ever been my greatest attribute. I've always had what my family would call "selective memory."

Or a vivid imagination.

Pointing has become my latest aerobic activity, and whatchamacallit is my noun of choice these days.

My remembrances of those halcyon days of childhood in Wisconsin are never quite the same as the rest of my family's.

When my older sister Lisa and I were about seven and eight we took swimming classes at the "Y" downtown.

I can still recall the scent of chlorine and the sound of twelve pairs of bare little-girl feet slip-slapping on the wet hardwood floor alongside the pool as we made our way to the dreaded diving board.

We looked like a pack of penguins in our shiny one-piece black bathing suits and white rubber swim caps strapped snugly beneath our chins. Those tightly stretched skull caps gave off an overpowering rubber smell, which in concert with the chlorine was a potent combination, enough to make a young girl swoon—particularly if she hadn't had her afternoon snack yet.

Maybe that helps to explain what happened next.

Perhaps I was a little faint from all the "Y" aromas swirling about me so that when it came my turn to dive off the board, I wasn't in perfect form. (Actually, I'm never in perfect form when diving—I prefer the one-handed jump method where my hand plugs my nose tightly shut to prevent water from whooshing up it.)

But that was many years later.

On this fateful day I was trying to be a good little girl and follow the diving directions.

Crack.

I hit my head on the bottom of the pool and had to be pulled to safety by the swimming instructor.

No wonder I'm not a water baby.

Years later, we were over at my folks' house one day when I first told my beloved about this traumatic childhood experience, and my mom burst out laughing.

Between snickers, she said, "Laura, that was ME. *You* never hit your head on the bottom of the pool when you were little—I did."

I'm really close to my mom so I guess I must have absorbed her childhood pain as my own.

See what they mean? Selective memory.

But at least that's better than no memory at all—which is what I have these days.

I'll get up from my desk to go to the kitchen for a glass of water, but halfway there, I forget what I got up for.

Can you relate?

Or I'll stride purposefully into the living room intending to pick up my latest *Victoria* magazine for a little soak-in-the-tub reading, and this time I'll make it all the way into the room before mentalpause hits.

So there I stand, wearing only a towel and a blank look.

Michael, however, wears an entirely different look.

Men and their one-track minds. At least he still has his mind.

But just wait 'til he turns forty.

True confession time: At the beginning of this chapter I told you I was forty-two. Now I've never been one of those women who lie about their age. And I'm not now.

I just forgot that I'm forty-three.

Must have been a mentalpause moment.

Either that or this age thing is moving much faster than I realized.

But at least I'm in good company.

Judi Braddy, a writer friend and pastor's wife, says when it comes to staying on track, her mentalpause train keeps getting derailed.

"I'm even beginning to think some of the spikes are missing," she confides. "For instance, a recent conversation with a friend went something like this: 'Oh, I have to tell you what I found today. You won't believe it! You know Jack Fritz, the guy who has done all the research on our denomination's early years . . . by the way, his parents attend a church where we visited two weeks ago . . . that was the greatest trip . . . we finally got to see that display that my husband was so interested in . . . although I can't believe how much it costs now compared to the last time we were there . . . you wouldn't believe how expensive the restaurants were! But the weather was great . . .'

"Now what was it that I wanted to tell you again?"

Loooooong pause.

"Well, if I think of it, I'll call you. But do you mind giving me your phone number again? I've forgotten it."

Then there's my friend Maria (with a Ph.D. and a bunch of other letters after her name) who teaches psychology in college. She admits that she's had more than her share of mentalpause moments in the classroom.

"I KNOW what I want to say, and something completely different comes out of my mouth," she says in frustration. "Like, I'm talking about the Oedipal complex and how it was based on *Oedipus Rex,* an ancient play written by . . . and then 'Shakespeare' comes out of my mouth when I KNOW it's Sophocles! And I KNOW it even while I'm saying 'Shakespeare.'

"It's as though my mind is saying 'it's an S word for author,' and I produce the one I use the most, even though it's not accurate and not what I mean to say."

Maria can take comfort in the fact that most of us probably wouldn't know the difference anyway.

She says that at least she puts those classroom mentalpause moments to good use.

"I suggest this is what we mean when we say the brain acts like a computer with a program that gives us the most-used answer right away after you only type in a few letters. . . ."

My cousin Susie Dayton also compares her brain to a computer.

"If my response seems slow when asked a question, I always explain: 'It is because I have numerous files and subfiles to sort through in order to retrieve the info . . . please stand by. Help . . . my computer needs more memory!'"

Even Michael suffers from mentalpause.

He says he needs one of those little hourglasses that comes up on the computer screen and says "processing" when someone asks him a question.

Or better yet, a blinking light like the Borg.

For those of you who aren't Star Trek fans, the Borg are bald, chalk-white robotic aliens—part-human, mostly machine—with all sorts of tubes and wires sticking out of their bodies and a light on their heads that blinks when they're assimilating information.

Wait a minute . . . that's the ticket. Everyone over forty just needs to get a blinking Borg light.

Then when they're having a mentalpause moment, at least people will know they're not lost in space on some distant planet.

Bright youth passes swiftly as a thought.

THEOGNIS

two

Who Is That Woman in the Mirror?

Where's my face and
what have you done with it?

If God had to give a woman wrinkles,
He might at least have put them on the soles of her feet.

NINON DE LENCLOS

Ever look in the mirror and not recognize yourself?

The first time this happened to me, I was in the hospital for my third chemo treatment for breast cancer.

By this stage, I was completely bald, and it was certain that no snowflakes would be staying on my nose and eyelashes, since I didn't have any—eyelashes, that is.

I didn't have any eyebrows either.

Definitely not one of my favorite things.

Plus, I'd burst a blood vessel in my eyes during an extended upchuck session.

Do you know what happens when you burst a blood vessel in your eye? Your eye completely fills up with blood.

It doesn't hurt though—not at all.

Really.

But it sure looks gross.

So it was no wonder I didn't recognize myself in the mirror that morning.

But that was nearly nine years ago, so what's my excuse now?

It's called middle age.

I never thought of myself as middle-aged until the day I heard two coworkers in their early twenties talk about some "middle-aged" woman who'd just been in the office. "She's at *least* forty," they were saying.

"Forty's not middle-aged," I sputtered indignantly. "I'm forty-three!"

While my mind refused to consider middle age, my body belied me.

I've always had a smooth, creamy complexion that I've kind of taken for granted. In fact, people used to tell me I could have been a model for those Dove bar ads.

Dove soap, ladies.

Get your mind out of the chocolate.

So it came as a real shock to me the day I discovered a fine layer of golden down—peach fuzz—covering my face.

I've always enjoyed classical music, but the term *long-hair* now holds new meaning.

I didn't recognize myself in the mirror—not with all this facial hair. It was so long I could have combed or even French-braided it. At least it was light-colored, which was more than I could say for my mustache AND the single dark-brown chin hair—AKA whisker—I suddenly sported.

Someone needs to prepare women for this unexpected furry dilemma.

Maybe I'll teach a class called "Women and Whiskers during the Pre-Twilight Years." We'll even have a theme song:

Sung to the tune of "The Gambler"

You gotta know when to bleach 'em
Know when to shave 'em,
Know when to use the Nair,
And know when to run.
You never pluck your chin hairs
When you're sittin' at the table;
There'll be time enough for pluckin'
In the bathroom mir'r.

Hair isn't the only thing to sprout on a woman's face after forty.

Cathy Evans says her young adult daughter keeps harping on her to "get with the times" and lose her bangs.

"Mom!" she exclaims. "Bangs are from the '80s."

"Shannon," Cathy replies, "my bangs are hiding major lines on my forehead, and I'm not about to get rid of them."

I've always enjoyed classical music, but the term longhair now holds new meaning.

But then one day when Cathy was looking in the mirror, she pulled her bangs away from her forehead and was astonished to find that the lines were almost completely gone. "Wow," she thought as she picked up the new bottle of moisturizing cream she'd recently purchased. "This is miracle stuff!"

It took her weeks to catch on to why the lines in her forehead had relaxed so much.

"A closer look in the mirror revealed something I hadn't realized before," recalled Cathy. "My eyebrows are lower now and, wait a minute . . . my eyelids look a little droopy.

"It's called gravity. It stretched out my forehead all right, but, help—my face is falling!"

In Eve Dorf's case, it isn't the face in the mirror she doesn't recognize, it's the face in the window over her kitchen sink.

"When daylight savings time goes away, I see myself again: Ooooh—gray hair and bifocals! I'm looking like my mother-in-law. My boys have told me how Grandma and I look so much alike in photos. Thanks.

"At least I get a reprieve all summer from my reflection."

Susie's reprieve comes in the form of a light switch.

"For years our master bathroom has had a dimmer on the light switch," she says. "That way, in the morning, it is not so much of a shock on the eyes after being in total darkness all night. But the dimmer now serves a dual purpose—it keeps me from the shock of seeing myself before my makeup is on.

"I have now perfected putting my 'face' on in the dimmest of light."

Except when it comes to mascara.

"My eyelashes were once long and curved, but now it takes a magnifying glass—or is it my eyesight—just to find them so I can paint them back on," Susie adds. "It's a major crisis when I run out of mascara and need to make a public appearance at the local K-Mart for a new tube."

She should have *my* problem.

One of the benefits of being an author is doing radio and TV interviews to promote your book. So a couple days before my first appearance on a national TV show, I visited my hairdresser for a trim and style that would look good on television.

I've always had thin hair, but as I've gotten older, it's started thinning even more—especially after undergoing chemo. I keep it short to give it more thickness and bounce.

Before I left on my trip back East, my hairdresser gave me a brand-new style and a little more height than I was accustomed to—but it very effectively covered the baby bald spot smack in the middle of the top of my head, which was a good thing.

Although it wasn't big hair, it was definitely poufy and looked like more hair than I'd had in years. I was quite pleased with the voluminous effect.

Two days later when I sat down in the backstage makeup chair, I felt like Julia Roberts getting the movie star treatment, and the *Pretty Woman* tune started running through my head.

But the music came to a screeching halt when the makeup girl casually pushed my painstakingly arranged bangs off my forehead to apply foundation.

I had spent nearly an hour in front of the hotel mirror that morning to re-create my new "do," so I was a little nervous when she kept pushing it off my face and behind my ears to do my makeup.

My fears were forgotten, however, when I saw the great job she did with my face: My eyes really stood out, and better yet, I had cheekbones—something I thought had been lost forever.

I was one happy guest.

Until she combed all the volume out of my carefully constructed hairstyle—leaving me with flat hair plastered to my scalp.

"Um . . . I think we need to pouf it up a bit more," I said weakly.

"Oh, not for TV," she said knowingly. "Your hair's so thin you can see right through it, and it would just show up as a lot of holes on camera."

So wouldn't that be a good thing since this was a Christian TV show?

Holey hair.

I always try to see the spiritual in everything, good not-so-little Christian girl that I am.

Judi's also a good Christian girl who thought she was having some sort of heavenly visitation when she looked in the mirror a few months ago.

"My mom passed away ten years ago," she said, "but just recently I was shocked to see her face in my mirror! Then I realized that it was not her at all but me. Somewhere along the path of my daily business, I had entered midlife and suddenly, mysteriously, turned into my mother.

"I bent forward to look more closely at the creases, crinkles, and double chin. I swear they were not there yesterday. How did this happen?" she asked.

It's called time—marching relentlessly across the face, leaving tread marks and wrinkles in its wake.

But that's okay.

I'd rather look like my mom any day than go back to those bald, Uncle Fester (*The Addams Family*) days from chemo.

The best mirror is an old friend.

GEORGE HERBERT

three

The Drop Zone

I've only just begun . . .
to sag.

Age is something that doesn't matter,
unless you are a cheese.

BILLIE BURKE

I don't know about you, but I've never been very ath-letic—ever since I twisted my ankle dismounting from the balance beam in seventh-grade gym class.

Sure, I was on the high school drill team, but marching isn't the most strenuous of sports.

Although it certainly came in handy during Air Force basic training.

I've just always preferred mental gymnastics to physi-cal—beginning way back in elementary school when I read 103 books in Miss Vopelinsky's first-grade class.

For me, working out is lifting *Gone with the Wind* or any James Michener novel from the bookcase.

And the only iron I pump is the one I use to press my clothes—once or twice a year.

For me, working out is lifting
Gone with the Wind or any James
Michener novel from the bookcase.

It's not my fault though. It's genetic.

I come from a pretty sedentary family.

Both my mom's and my sister's favorite physical activ-ity is bingo.

Speaking of my sister, Lisa—did I mention she's older than I am? Well, she got a little scare recently.

She'd just gotten out of the shower and was toweling off in front of her steamed-up full-length bathroom mirror when she noticed something unusual hanging down between her legs.

Bewildered and a little concerned, since cancer runs in our family, she quickly donned her glasses and wiped off the mirror to better identify the offending object.

Heavy sigh of relief. It wasn't a tumor.

It was just her derriere.

Dropped derriere. Another unexpected benefit of "middle age" but not one I'd ever heard discussed in polite company before.

After Lisa called to tell me this story, I rushed to the mirror and dropped my jeans to see if I shared the same malady.

Whew! Saved by the thunder thighs. (Words I never ever thought I'd use together in the same sentence.) But in this instance, they provided a tightly closed curtain that effectively blocked the dropped-derriere view.

No such luck with my breasts.

There's no nearby body part I could use to block the sight of those dropped puppies.

It wasn't always so.

Remember back in high school when we took the pencil test?

We all proudly took our No. 2 pencils and placed them beneath our budding bosoms. Naturally, they (the pencils) all clattered to the floor—except for the D-cup girl's. And we all wore a look of triumph that we had passed this significant test of perky beauty.

When my friend Karen did the pencil test, she said that not only could she keep the pencil in place, but she could even lift up the coffee table.

That's why she now wears a bra minimizer.

I haven't taken the test in years. So in the interest of research (see what I'm willing to do for you, dear reader?) I think I'll take it right now. Give me just a minute.

Waaa-aaah. I failed.

I'm so depressed. I NEVER, ever fail tests.

Math doesn't count.

Wait a sec. Let me take it again—just to be sure.

Yippee! This time I passed.

I knew I could. I knew I could.

Gotta love those saline implants.

Okay, I cannot tell a lie. So one side failed and the other one passed—with flying colors, I might add—but in my book, if you average out an A and an F, you come up with a passing grade of C.

It's not just bosoms and bottoms that start sagging as we get older.

There's also that wonderful under-the-arm swing most of us develop.

Karen Grant still remembers her grade school teacher Mrs. Jennings writing on the chalkboard with her arms flapping furiously in the wind.

"She knocked out a little boy in the front row with those babies," Karen quipped.

I'm afraid we're all in for the flapping arms—unless we get filthy rich and can hire personal trainers to fight them. Although, on her show, even Oprah's admitted—and shown—that *she* has them.

Guess you just can't fight Mother Nature.

But you *can* disguise her handiwork.

That's why most of us cleverly conceal our flabby upper arms with long-sleeved shirts, blouses, or dresses. And when we wear T-shirts, it's always the kind where the sleeves come down to the elbow.

Those cute little cap-sleeved T-shirts we wore in our twenties?

Forget it.

And sleeveless? Not on your life.

I haven't appeared sleeveless in public in twenty years.

Until that fateful day I went shopping at Nordstrom.

I'd never shopped at Nordstrom before in my life because it just wasn't in my budgetsphere. Generally, I'm a Target, JCPenney, or Gottschalk's gal—with the occasional visit to Macy's basement.

But this was something special. I was about to embark on my very first book tour, preceded by a visit to a booksellers convention.

In New Orleans.

In July.

Have you ever been to New Orleans in July?

Can you say sauna?

It was important that I look good but also that I be able to breathe.

So, a few weeks before the trip, Mom, my aunt Mary, and my best friend Lana and I went on the shopping trip to end all shopping trips—during the Nordstrom semiannual sale.

Lana and Mary are the shopping queens.

They really know how to work a room.

Mom and Mary started in one corner of the store downstairs in Petites, while little Lana graciously rode the escalator with me up to the larger women's section called Encore—a classier word for MORE.

I had an idea what I wanted . . . a couple classic pieces with long, slimming lines, preferably in jewel tones. With my Scandinavian complexion—think pale, although Michael, bless his heart, calls it "creamy"—I look best in vivid fuschia, ruby red, sapphire blue, or emerald green.

And I never, ever, do tan or beige.

But then I spotted a gorgeous summer pantsuit with the long slimming lines I was seeking.

Only problem was, it was beige.

And sleeveless.

Now, any woman over forty (other than Goldie Hawn or Lauren Hutton) can tell you that you never, ever wear sleeveless outfits.

Yet this pantsuit was so classic and rich, and Lana kept pushing me to try it on, so I finally caved.

And you know what?

I looked absolutely fabulous, dahling.

Old habits die hard though, and I bought the beautiful beige pantsuit with the understanding that I'd find a nice chocolate brown T-shirt to wear under it to hide my bigger-than-a-breadbasket white arms.

While Lana tried on a couple more outfits, I went in search of my mom and aunt to show them my find.

Aunt Mary is a strikingly beautiful woman with long, naturally curly jet-black hair who turns heads whenever she walks into a room. No one can believe she's in her fifties—especially men. She looks more like thirty, so it's kind of annoying to go out in public with her.

But we love her, so we make the sacrifice.

Mary was trying on a gorgeous white pantsuit—also sleeveless—that looked wonderful on her, especially against her sun-bronzed skin. When I complimented her on it, she said, "But I'd have to wear a T-shirt under it—I can't ever wear sleeveless with these arms."

None of the women in my family were about to break the no-sleeveless rule.

That's why when I got home I tried on dozens of T-shirts and short-sleeved blouses beneath my new beige suit—in front of Carolyn, a costume designer friend of ours who'd come over for dinner.

I finally had to throw out the T-shirt.

"It ruins the whole line of the outfit," Carolyn said. "Just go sleeveless."

Sacrilege.

Especially to a big-armed, pasty-skinned woman.

When I complained about my white fat showing, she said, "Just use some tan in a bottle."

I'd heard of Time in a Bottle, but tan in a bottle?

I had vague, unpleasant memories of some cheapie stuff we tried in junior high that made our skin turn orange.

But Carolyn assured me that liquid tanning had come a long way since then, and everyone—including Estee Lauder and Clinique—had now jumped on the tan-wagon.

So I slathered on a little Island Gold, borrowed Lana's leopard print scarf, and voila!

Look out, New Orleans, here I come.

Michael appreciated the effect.

But my husband—who's been an actor and stage manager and knows all the tricks to use onstage—knew I was still a little arm-nervous, so he gave me a reassuring tip.

"Honey, just try to keep your arms close to your sides; don't gesture so much and then they won't flap."

Now that's what I call true love.
Or no fear.
Or stupidity.

I praise you because I am fearfully and wonderfully made.

PSALM 139:14

four

PMS Is a Picnic in the Park

It ends after a few days,
but menopause just keeps on goin'.

The secret of staying younger is to live honestly, eat slowly, and just not think about your age.

LUCILLE BALL

They call it menopause.

Perimenopause. Personally, I prefer Perry Como. (For those of you under thirty, go ask your mom who he is.)

Perimenopause. Personally, I prefer Perry Como. (For those of you under thirty, go ask your mom who he is.)

Perimenopause is just the beginning stages of menopause—which can last anywhere from two to five years.

So far, I'm just a little past the one-year mark.

My friend Peggy says she has "graduated" from premenstrual syndrome to perimenopausal syndrome.

"What fun! If I follow in the footstep of my female relatives, all this will be over in two years or so," she says.

But perimenopause and menopause make PMS look like a picnic in the park.

"PMS is very predictable—time-wise," says my sister-in-law Sheri, who just turned fifty.

Her forty-seven-year-old friend M. J. agrees: "There's at least a cycle there."

Ken, whose wife Pat went through a very difficult menopause that lasted nearly five years, seconds that.

"I can do PMS standing on my head," he says. "I knew when it was coming and what to expect. After just five or six days, it was gone 'til the next month. But menopause just keeps on going and going!"

Like the Eveready bunny.

"PMS came without fail every twenty-eight days," said Judi. "I could see it coming and yell: 'Back away and no one gets hurt!'

"However, the moods of menopause are like the Midwestern thunderstorms of my youth: They build up suddenly and without notice, rain on anyone unlucky enough to be caught in their path, and strike terror in the hearts of those who've never experienced them before."

The whole menopause/PMS thing baffles Trisha.

"I read that if you have serious PMS you can expect to have a difficult change of life," she says. "Is that fair?!

"I've watched female family members skate through life with no PMS, then skate through menopause as well. It seems like they should have to pay their dues at some point," she grumbles.

"I suffered from PMS all my life—our whole life was planned around it—then began menopause in my early forties.

"Menopause, or in my case, perimenopause, was like having one very long bout of PMS—a situation you wouldn't wish on your worst enemy," Trisha says.

But she's able to look on the bright side now. "I watch my newly married son handle his wife's PMS with such aplomb after a lifetime of practice," she says proudly.

My friend Carolyn White, who went through menopause about a decade ago, said that women in her family never talked about the "M" word.

"They especially never used the word, as though it were unseemly," she said with a smile. "Most of my women friends were younger than me and not experiencing anything similar. So I was alone in this and didn't really know what it was. No one mentioned such an unmentionable word in the media, and I had never seen any books or magazine articles about it that connected this condition to what I was experiencing."

Carolyn says her menopause experience was memorable because it was in tandem with a writing project she was doing at the time—under a very tight deadline.

"The designer and I were pulling all-nighters week after week," she said. "I remember sitting at my computer keyboard at three in the morning, printing out copy on my laser printer, perspiration dripping down my back and off my nose, windows open, a fan going, my internal 'thermostat' waaaay out of whack, and I'm thinking . . . *boy, I know I'm sensitive to the toner in my laser printer, but this must be chemical madness going on here.*

"I would have been more alarmed for my health under what I was convinced must be environmentally unsafe conditions—something like writing a book called *Chernobyl Meets the China Syndrome*—but I was under such laughably unreal deadlines that I couldn't allow myself to think about it," she recalls. "I was writing and printing out chapter after chapter, draft after draft, as fast as I could, convinced I was sealing my doom with black lung disease.

"I was also newly married and totally out of touch with the fact that this could be menopause—a word I never imagined murmuring across the breakfast table with my new and very sexy husband.

"When I fell into bed after those all-nighters, I was mortified to awaken with soaked sheets, hoping my sweet, sleeping husband might not notice. How he could not notice my soaking wet body and soaking wet not-so-sexy-anymore nightgown, I don't know.

"After living with this for about a year, I finally found ONE book in the bookstore about menopause," Carolyn said. "I bought it, read it, and figured out what was going on. My doctor put me on hormone treatments and most of the craziness went away."

Not every woman goes through a difficult menopause.

Eve Dorf, a fellow breast cancer survivor, says she "loves" menopause.

"No more cramps, surprises, and most of all, no more PMS.

"I have no mood swings," she reports happily. "Only moments—senior, chemo, Tamoxifen—of lost vocabulary and hot flashes."

Joyce Pope said she finally realized there is a positive side to all of this hormonal change: "I don't ever have to deal with menses again.

"I was truly reminded of this one summer when my four daughters were home as well as a female friend and a female cousin.

"Unfortunately, they all cycled at the same time."

Joyce found herself wishing she had a cycle too—a bicycle—so she could pedal away from this not very pleasant PMS party.

Over the years, I've subjected Michael to plenty of unhappy PMS parties as well.

Beginning in our dating days.

But since he proposed marriage to me during a particularly emotional PMS attack, I figure he knew what he was getting himself into.

For everything God created is good, and nothing is to be rejected if it is received with thanksgiving.
1 TIMOTHY 4:4

five

Thermostat Wars

Is it hot in here,
or is it just me?

She's no chicken; she's on the wrong side of thirty
if she be a day.

JONATHAN SWIFT

Over the course of her thirty-two-year marriage to Chuck, Susie says they've had continuous "thermostat wars."

"For the first twenty-plus years, I was always turning the heat up and Chuck the opposite," she recalls. "But for the past ten years, *I'm* the one turning the heat down and he's the one who's freezing!"

I've got Susie beat.

I can turn the thermostat up, then down again, in a matter of minutes.

Michael calls it my three-degree-temperature-tolerance range.

I'm most comfortable when it's between sixty-nine and seventy-one degrees—inside or out. Otherwise, I'm either BOILING hot or FREEZING cold.

I'm forever going to the thermostat—which my honey has programmed to kick in when we get up in the morning and turn off when we go to bed at night—and punching it up a couple degrees higher when I'm cold.

Ten minutes later, when I feel as if I'm going to ABSOLUTELY SUFFOCATE from the heat, I knock the thermostat down a couple notches to cool off.

Guess that's why Michael calls me his woman of extremes.

I hate to be hot.

At least when it's cold, you can always bundle on more clothes and snuggle cozily beneath a quilt.

Heat doesn't work that way: There are only so many clothes you can take off.

Just another reason summer is my least favorite season.

In fact, I hate the sun.

This from a woman who lives in sun-drenched California.

Not only California but also the state capital—Sacramento—which in the summer is known for its sizzling temperatures of 100 and above. I joined the Air Force to get out of one hot climate—Phoenix—but since Sacramento's now home, I'm learning to adapt.

It's called air-conditioning.

There are only so many clothes you can take off.

Sunshine and temperatures in the 90s and above are for people who enjoy outdoor sports—particularly those that involve water: swimming, waterskiing, beach volleyball.

I don't do water unless it's a tub full of Calgon.

Besides, this body hasn't wriggled into a bathing suit in fifteen years.

And although I don't mind the neighbors seeing me in shorts while I'm out watering the lawn, I won't venture farther than the perimeter of my block in them.

The water is also home to sharks, my mortal enemy, thanks to *Jaws*.

For years after seeing that movie, I refused to go in the ocean—convinced that Mighty Mouth was just lying in wait for my tender white skin—even in the shallow waters right off shore.

Don't tell me sharks don't come in that close.

I saw the movie.

They also said birds never attack. I've seen that movie too.

Now, don't get the wrong idea and think I'm a big baby. I'm actually quite adventurous. Well . . . was. By the time I was twenty-three, I'd visited sixteen countries outside of the United States.

One memorable trip was a vacation to Greece that I took while stationed in England. Since I was traveling alone, the tour guide had me bunk with two girls from Australia.

Problem was, Australian girls like to swim.

Comes from living on an island, I guess.

Part of our tour involved visiting three Greek islands: Hydra, Poros, and Aegina. All those color posters you see of pristine white buildings against a sapphire sea are dazzlingly true-to-life. There's a glorious, almost primitive beauty to the Greek isles.

While my two water baby friends were cavorting in the turquoise-blue of the Mediterranean, I was blissfully sunning on the beach.

They kept pleading with me to join them in the ocean, but I was adamant, reminding them of my *Jaws* phobia. After forty-five minutes of broiling in the sun, however, I could no longer resist the water's inviting coolness.

So I finally took the plunge, paddling around for a bit with my sea nymph friends, then just floating lazily on my back.

Suddenly, without warning, Mr. Big Jaws attacked.

My legs were violently pulled under and my whole body followed in short order.

That's when I heard the creepy *Jaws* music—bum-bum, bum-bum—hummed by my Aussie friends.

I haven't been swimming in the ocean since.

Sure, I'll take romantic walks on the beach with Michael—even bravely barefoot through the incoming tide—but there's no way I'm going any farther than that.

I don't do water and I don't do heat, which has been a bit of a problem in our marriage as far as deciding where to live.

Over the years, I've fantasized about moving to the cooler climate in the Midwest—where housing prices just happen to be much lower than California. But Michael can't handle cold weather, and he knew *he'd* be the one stuck shoveling snow, so there went that fantasy.

For now, we're happy to stay in Sacramento.

Even though we have hot, hot summers, it doesn't really affect me since I don't do outdoor activities.

The funny thing lately is that Michael—who works all day long in an air-conditioned office—can't handle the heat now either.

And I can't handle the cold.

They say that after you've been married long enough, you start to take on the characteristics of your spouse.

Michael's becoming more like me, and vice versa.

Or maybe we're just getting older?

Thermostat wars are not just the province of married couples.

When Karen was living in an apartment in New York City with her friend Stephanie, she came home one day to find her roommate huddled in a chair and wearing her coat and gloves.

"We have to put the heat on, Karen," Stephanie wailed. "It's *freezing* in here."

Karen, who was going through major menopausal hot flashes at the time, replied, "Just put on another sweater."

Jill does just the opposite.

Her elderly mother lives with her and thinks it's cold when the thermostat reads under 75. So Jill just sheds more clothing when her mom turns up the heat. "People sort of stare when I answer the door in the dead of winter in shorts and a T-shirt."

Maria has both Jill and Karen beat.

"In South Dakota, where the nighttime temperatures drop below freezing six months out of the year, I slept six inches from a north-facing window that was kept open at all times," Maria recalled.

"One night I awoke because something was tickling my nose . . . snow!

"It was covering my face, my pillow, and most of my husband, Ralph, who was completely inside his down comforter. I laughed until I cried. It was such a funny picture. You would have thought we were camping.

"I still bless my husband for putting up with it," said Maria, "although he learned to 'sleep better' with cold too. Isn't that a sign of love?"

Cold nose, warm heart . . .

What do we live for, if it is not to make life less difficult for each other?

GEORGE ELIOT

six

I'm Havin' a Heat Wave

Those hot flashes sure aren't pretty—
or going away anytime soon.

If you can't stand the heat, get out of the kitchen.

HARRY S. TRUMAN

I've been having lots of heat waves lately. And they're anything but tropical.

I try to take it all in stride—especially when I'm out in public. But it's kind of difficult when the top half of my body is burning up and all I want to do is tear off all my clothes and jump in the nearest body of water.

Swimming pool. Stagnant pond. Bird bath.

Karen Graham discovered a great water solution for her menopausal wave.

"I was sitting in a very fancy restaurant with dear friends, and as the maitre d' walked by, suddenly a hot flash hit," she recalled. "Without thinking twice, I poured an entire glass of ice water down my back.

"The maitre d' stopped and asked, 'Is everything okay here?'

"'Why, of course. What would make you think otherwise?' I said with a smile while water dripped onto the beautiful damask tablecloth and my friends attempted to act like nothing was out of the ordinary.

"I felt soooo much better," Karen recalled.

"He just raised a French eyebrow and scurried away. Of course, the service for our table declined ever so much."

Another friend of mine, also named Karen, has a perfect solution for hot flashes: "I strip off as much as I can as quickly as I can without drawing attention to myself. Of course, it depends on who you're around. You can't strip down in front of a lot of people and not have them question you—especially in a public place. . . . 'H'mmm, she came in wearing a dress; now she's just in a slip.'"

Karen also recommends wearing layers of clothes. "Don't ever just wear a bulky sweater unless you plan on stripping down to your bra when a flash hits."

Jill from Wisconsin agrees.

"So much for all those terrific wool sweaters and turtlenecks you have in all colors. Plan on a rummage sale— you won't need them anymore."

Forgoing sweaters and turtlenecks isn't an infallible solution however.

Hot flashes can strike in a second and turn you into an instant Gypsy Rose Lee even when you're as minimally clothed as modesty will allow.

"If I can get only one article of clothing off and it can't be my T-shirt, it has to be my bra," says Karen. "I've been talking to people and I pull it right out—from beneath my blouse—and they say, 'Whoa, how bohemian.'"

"No, menopausal."

Been there, done that.

Discreetly, of course. And never in mixed company— other than Michael.

Sometimes I barely make it through the front door before I'm whipping my bra off.

And if I've got something else on my mind at the time— like putting away groceries—I'll just drop it on the nearest surface and forget about it.

Couch.

Chair.

Dining room table.

"Oh, are we having prosthesis for dinner tonight?" asks Michael. "I prefer chicken."

Humor can be a wonderful weapon in the hot flash war— if wielded properly.

Electric fans are a safer bet.

Jill and her middle-school colleague are about the same age. The two women keep a fan in their small office and frequently make visits to it throughout the day to cool down.

"You can be standing there teaching and all of a sudden, it feels like someone lit a fire under you," relates Jill. "It starts from the waist and moves up until you can feel the sweat running down your back; then your forehead beads up and you wish you could get to any place where it's cold.

"And it's always nice when your palms sweat so much that the pens you're using on the overhead projector smear and run.

"Kids have asked why I seem to be sweating so much," Jill adds. "I just tell them it's because I'm working so hard to educate them."

Susie, a nurse, says she doesn't know what she would have done at work without the hot flash fan that her friend Bonnie sent her for one of her landmark birthdays.

"As the intense, almost inescapable heat entraps me, I get welcome relief with that little fan," she reports. "My coworkers are always quick to loudly announce, 'Sue's having a flash.' My desperation must be more obvious than I think as I rip off my lab coat, unbutton my collar, and roll up my sleeves."

A lab coat was Karen's salvation.

Also a nurse, she was home on call one day when she was paged to return to the senior care hospital where she works. It was an emergency, so Karen dashed over immediately in the clothes she was wearing—a pair of khaki pants and a turtleneck.

When she got there, the turtleneck began to suffocate her.

"Because the majority of older patients have thyroid problems, they're always cold, so the thermostats are kept set at 80 or 90 degrees," she explained.

Suddenly strangling, Karen whipped off the turtleneck, donned a lab coat—which she had to pin up since it was too low cut—and was ready to offer the tender loving care her patient needed.

All menopausal women could do with a little TLC since so few are immune from the hot flash horrors. Although to some, they're "warm waves" instead.

"I'll be at my desk doing absolutely nothing," says Merrie, "and suddenly my forehead and upper lip burst out in a sweat. I always think I'm getting the flu; I'll ask, 'Do I have a fever?'"

Merrie even had to change her hairstyle—she's added bangs—to disguise her office sweats.

That wouldn't help Lonnie.

"I don't sweat below the neck when I'm having a hot flash," she confides. "Nothing under my arms, just the hair on my head—soaking wet."

Recently, however, it was more than just her hair.

After she finished working out at the gym, Lonnie told her personal trainer, "It feels good to sweat from something other than a hot flash."

"He laughed and laughed," she recalled. "I don't think he knows many menopausal women."

Menopausal Karen's hot flashes start right below her sternum—the very core center of her being—and go straight up in an explosion. "It's really embarrassing when it shows," she says. "My face gets flaming red and my nose stays red longer than any other part.

"Just call me Rudolph."

Holidays can really turn up the hot flash heat.

My cousin Barb Colwell recalls one Thanksgiving when she was about thirteen; her mom (my aunt Lucille) and a close family friend the kids all called Aunt Kay were busy cooking dinner in the kitchen.

"The kitchen was not very big, and the oven had been going for hours cooking that big bird," she said. "Mom opened the oven door to give it another basting, and within seconds she and Aunt Kay ran to the back door and stuck their heads out, waving their shirts out around them like fans. I remember thinking how funny they looked, but I was also a little confused; it wasn't *that* hot in there.

"*Now* I understand," she said knowingly.

Barb later married a man eleven years her senior—Frank—who had sisters ten years his senior. "One time we went up north for a family reunion, and his sisters were all busily preparing for it—cleaning, scrubbing, and cooking," she recalls. "I watched as one by one they started to perspire profusely—especially around the hairlines. They were simply dripping wet! But they just wrapped towels around their heads and kept on working.

"I couldn't help but wonder what kind of gene they inherited that made them sweat so, but I was sure glad it didn't run in *our* family," Barb said. "Lo and behold, about ten or twelve years later, I'm working around the house one day and I start sweating like crazy around the hairline. 'It's not a gene, it's menopause,' I decided."

Cousin Susie always sleeps with the windows wide open—no matter what time of the year—and one foot hanging out from under the covers. "This is so I have a head start on escaping when a flash hits in the night," she explains.

Even worse than the hot flashes are the night sweats.

"I have four pairs of pajamas that are ready at all times," says Karen. "Most nights now I go through two pairs."

Sue Lenart said her first mistake was having a male gynecologist who thought she was exaggerating when she told him her nightly routine: "I put on my nightgown and place a second nightgown at the foot of the bed. Then I place a Kleenex box nearby.

"When I wake up with the night sweats, I take off the soaked nightgown, put on the dry one—get chilled in the process—grab the Kleenex, and try to make it to the bathroom before the violent sneezing causes my overly full bladder to explode."

I've been fortunate thus far to bypass the night sweats. But last summer, I had a day sweat that was pretty horrible.

I'd accompanied Michael to his company picnic, which was held at a local water park on a hot summer day. He was really looking forward to having fun with his coworkers . . . I was looking forward to trying to stay cool.

The good thing is that we've now been married long enough to know what works for us and what doesn't. My staying outside in the sun and heat for a long period of time doesn't.

So I wisely suggested we take two cars.

When we arrived, we looked for his friends, but when we couldn't find them, we headed straight for the food tables set up under awnings.

Unfortunately, there was no shade at the picnic tables where we were expected to eat. Just the scorching Sacramento sun beating down relentlessly.

I was really having a good time now.

Finally we spotted one of Michael's coworkers who motioned us over to a shady spot that she'd managed to snag under some trees.

Ah, blessed relief.

Until the bees started swarming us.

I kept swatting them away with one hand while trying to eat with my other hand and make small talk at the same time.

After about half an hour, I stood up and said, "Well, this has been fun, but I think I really need to be heading home now."

"Nice to meet you," I said politely to Michael's coworker. "Have fun, you guys. Love you, honey . . . see you later."

Then I kissed Michael good-bye and sprinted—okay, for me, that would be walked fast—to the parking lot.

Fifteen minutes later, I made it to my car, dripping sweat.

It was all I could do not to strip in the car on the way home. I did manage to undo my bra at a red light though.

The minute I walked in the house, I pulled the curtains shut tight, tore off all my clothes, punched the a/c down really low, parked my naked body—arms stretched over my head—in front of the standing fan in the bedroom, and blasted it on high.

After I finally cooled down—in fact, started to get a little chilly—I pulled on an all-cotton sundress, selected a movie from the den, made a nice soothing cup of Earl Grey, and hunkered down under a quilt for the rest of the afternoon with Anthony Hopkins, Emma Thompson, and *Howard's End*.

Now that's what I call a perfect way to spend a summer day.

Be content with what you have.
HEBREWS 13:5

seven

Playing Connect-the-Dots With My Age Spots

Overnight, small brown dots mysteriously appeared . . .
right above my middle-age spread.

Old age is like a plane flying through a storm. Once you're aboard, there's nothing you can do.

GOLDA MEIR

When I was young, I thought age spots only appeared on "older" people—say in their seventies and eighties.

Although what constitutes "older" has now changed a bit.

Middle age has definitely moved up to the higher end of the scale.

Now 60 is middle-aged. Hey, I've heard of people living to 120. It can happen.

I remember seeing age spots on my grandparents and figuring it was just a natural part of growing old—something I wouldn't have to worry about for years and years.

That's why it was such a shock when they first appeared on my chest.

Since I'm a breast cancer survivor, I always pay special attention to any changes in my chest area, so when these pale brown dots suddenly appeared, I grew concerned and made an appointment to see my doctor.

"Those are just age spots, Laura," he told me with a gentle smile.

"AGE spots? But I'm barely forty!"

"Some people get them earlier than others."

Well, *that* was a great comfort.

I'd been a late bloomer in most other areas of my life:

Not wearing a bra 'til I was fifteen and a half
First kiss at sixteen
Becoming a Christian at age twenty-seven
Marriage at thirty-four
College degree at thirty-five
First book published at forty

Why oh why couldn't my body cooperate with my delayed timetable? But no-o-o-o-o, my age spots had to sprout up like dandelions.

On the way home from the doctor's, I stopped by the grocery store to drown my sorrows in some chocolate-chip ice cream.

Those brown spots I can handle.

But the ones on my chest really took some getting used to.

It wasn't as if there were just one or two stray marks either. There were about a baker's dozen sprinkled across my chest.

And when I connected them, they formed the great state of Texas.

Do you know the song "Deep in the Heart of Texas"? Then sing along with me.

The dots at night
Are big and bright
(clap-clap-clap-clap)
Deep on the chest like Texas.

Don't tell me you never played that connect-the-dots game when you were a kid.

Or made up goofy songs. Here's another one (sung to the tune of "I've Been Workin' on the Railroad"):

> *I've got dots across my che-est*
> *All the livelong day.*
> *I've tried creams and lots of makeup*
> *Tryin' to make them go away.*
> *Dontcha see them fadin' fa-ast?*
> *Look, I think they're nearly gone!*
> *Drat, they're back, it didn't la-ast,*
> *They came back with the dawn.*

My friend Jean wants to know just when the back of her hands started looking like she remembers her grandmother's hands—or worse yet, her grandfather's—with the little brown spots that she thought was dirt when she was little.

In addition to age spots, there's an army of freckles that have also begun to march over my body willy-nilly. I've always had a few freckles here and there, but now that I've gotten older, I'm breaking out all over.

Good thing Michael thinks they're "cute."

Katie, a strawberry blonde, is covered with cute from head to toe. "I like freckles," she declares impishly. "I don't think I'll have to worry about any age spots."

For those of us who do, there is a bright side . . .

"When we're completely covered, we'll have a natural tan," says M. J.

Not willing to wait that long, my friend Judi is hoping Estee Lauder will soon make a bodysuit—with matching gloves—in cool beige.

I'm not the only one in my family with interesting spots.

My cousin Susie, who's in her early fifties, recounts, "After observing my arms recently and noticing the masses of white spots where pigment had once been, my six-year-old granddaughter Ashley exclaimed, 'Wow, Grandma! Look at all those polka dots. Cool!'"

Hey—perhaps if Susie connected all her dots she could form California on her arm. And maybe if my relatives and I all joined together with our spots, we could form a jigsaw puzzle of the whole Western United States.

Wouldn't it be great if we could form something besides fat on our tummies?

Unfortunately, there's a reason they call it middle-age spread.

"I've never had a problem until the last two years," pouts forty-eight-year-old Merrie. "Now I'm wider all the way around."

Me too.

So is Michael—which really makes it a challenge now when we kiss. It's almost like two sumo wrestlers bouncing off each other.

Wouldn't it be great if we could form something besides fat on our tummies?

"With menopause, the body changes no matter how slender you are," says Nurse Karen. "You can still have slender arms and legs, but your middle's definitely going to get bigger."

"The shoulders get bony, and the stomach gets softer," confirms Sheri.

Schoolteacher Jill was starting to wonder why her clothes didn't fit the same. "Everything feels tight," she complains. "The manufacturers must be cutting back on material; nothing seems to fit around the waist."

Maybe it has something to do with those chocolate supplements she's been taking in addition to her Hormone Replacement Therapy.

"My teaching partner and I have in our outer office a file drawer marked HEALTH," says Jill. "Want to guess what's in it? When people say chocolate takes on its own personality at this stage, believe them. I have colleagues who will kill for chocolate."

In our house, everyone knows that you touch my chocolate and die.

What once was a vice is now a necessity.

Although by the same token, what once gave me energy now just sits on my hips.

My tastes haven't changed, but my body has, unfortunately.

Including my feet.

Yes, my feet. They too have gotten bigger as I've gotten older.

Jill says she's read several books that positively state that feet can grow with the advent of the change of life.

Remember the sweaters and turtlenecks Jill plans to give away at the next rummage sale? Now she has thirty-two pairs of shoes waiting to join them.

From birth to age 18, a girl needs good parents, from 18 to 35 she needs good looks, from 35 to 55 she needs a good personality, and from 55 on she needs cash.

SOPHIE TUCKER

eight

Of Crow's Feet, Varicose Veins, and Facial Hair

One line leads to another.

Nature gives you the face you have at twenty; it is up to
you to merit the face you have at fifty.

COCO CHANEL

Varicose veins run in my family.

We'd like them to run away from home, but they're not leaving.

Oh well, maybe I'll finally learn to read road maps now that one's permanently etched on my legs.

Something's also come to roost on my face as well.

Crow's feet.

Whoever came up with the description "crow's feet" anyway?

I prefer laugh lines.

Oh well, maybe I'll finally learn to read road maps now that one's permanently etched on my legs.

In addition to crow's feet and varicose veins, another common malady of middle age is the dreaded double chin.

The first time I was to appear on a local TV show, I was bemoaning the fact that TV automatically adds ten pounds, and with my double chin, it would be more like twenty.

Michael, my ever-helpful Renaissance man, told me a way we could disguise my twin chins.

Since he used to work in a professional theater troupe, he knew a special trick older stage actors and actresses occasionally use to hide their double chins.

They take little pieces of invisible adhesive tape, stick them under their jaw line, attach invisible strings—usually fishing wire—and then tautly pull the strings and anchor them behind each ear.

Presto. No more double chin or pesky wrinkles either.

I was sorely tempted, but then I kind of thought it would be false advertising, so I decided against it. Besides, while this makeup special effects trick works well for the stage, the tape and string would have shown up on camera (and my skin doesn't respond well to adhesive tape either).

I may have drawn the line for TV, but I didn't mind crossing it when I posed for an all-important author photo.

"Chin up," the photographer directed.

Which one? I was tempted to ask.

Instead I just lifted my main chin first by tipping my head back ever so slightly. Then I carefully and discreetly anchored the second chin in place by jauntily resting the first one on my hand and tilting my head playfully to one side—all the while keeping a firm finger hold on Chin Number Two.

Oops; hope they don't make me turn in my author card for revealing this double-chinned "celebrity" secret.

Trisha's never had a double chin, but when she started going through menopause she did begin to break out with acne.

"I was battling age spots, crow's feet, and zits all at the same time," she said mournfully.

Faces aren't the only body part that feels the ravages of time.

Kat, who calls herself "a Prozac sister," says she's noticed as she gets older that her thighs tend to get "puffy."

Not fat.

Puffy.

Fat seems so permanent. Puffy can go down overnight.

To eliminate the puffiness, Kat does multiple leg lifts. "After each exercise session—like most women—I check my thighs in the mirror to see if they've gone down at all," she says.

"Then I walk back into the living room where I'd been exercising and fail to understand why there is no thigh matter laying on the floor like the retreads on the freeway that have fallen off an eighteen-wheeler's tires."

It's not only women who go through bodily changes with age.

Remember that great Billy Crystal line in *City Slickers*? "I'm losing hair where I *want* hair, and I'm getting hair where there shouldn't be hair."

Michael can vouch for that.

He's thinning on top—and bottom. (He's losing hair on his calves.)

And he's gaining hair . . . in his ears.

Good thing I'm handy with a tweezers.

Although I don't remember ear hair plucking being part of the marriage vows . . . guess that would fall under "for better or worse."

When Michael and I met more than a decade ago, he had a full head of dark brown hair and a nice dark beard with just one or two gray hairs. In the last couple years though, his hairline has receded a bit and his beard has become more salt than pepper.

One morning he came out of the bathroom looking downcast. "I'm turning gray everywhere," he complained. "I just trimmed a white hair from my nose!"

"That's okay, honey," I said giving him a big hug and batting my eyelashes flirtatiously. "If you don't mind my mustache, I don't mind your nose hair."

Many women have to contend with menopausal mustaches as they grow older.

Some wax it off, some pluck it, others shave it.

But Karen, my nurse friend, insists that bleach is best.

"Bleach—just remember bleach," she exhorts.

But make sure to remember to time how long you leave the bleach solution on.

Karen forgot once and wound up with a burned upper lip. "When you bleach you'll always feel a little burning or discomfort. I felt it but thought, *It's just doing its job.*"

When she looked in the mirror, she realized it had done that and much, much more.

Good thing she had plenty of concealer on hand.

Sister-in-law Sheri gets a shock sometimes when she walks by a mirror.

"I see a reflection in it and think, *Who's that?*"

In her mind she thinks she still looks like her twenty-one-year-old daughter. But when she looks in the mirror, she sees her grandma.

Karen sees her mother.

"When did this happen?" she asks. "I can dye my hair, wear purple eye shadow, and I still look like my mother."

Recently, I found out I looked like someone else's mother.

I was at a speaking engagement—which my mom also attended—and after introducing my mother to the group, one of the women piped up, "And is that your daughter?" pointing to a friend who'd also accompanied us.

"My DAUGHTER?" I said incredulously. "She's twenty-two! I'm not old enough to have a twenty-two-year-old daughter!"

Well, mathematically speaking, I guess I am.

But this was too much for my math-impaired brain to handle.

I'm not the only one who has trouble adding up the years.

When Jerry Bauman entered an airport hotel restaurant for breakfast one day near the end of a grueling business trip, he noticed a sign welcoming the "Merrill's Marauders Reunion."

"Trivia buff that I am, I remembered that this had been a commando unit operating behind Japanese lines in Burma during World War II," Jerry recalled. (He was about six or seven years old at the time the commandos were serving in the war.)

"As I finished my breakfast and asked the waitress for my bill, she asked me if I was part of the Merrill's Marauders group.

"Taken aback, I immediately said 'no,' then asked, 'How old do you think I *am?*'"

Maybe I should go back up to my room and look in the mirror, Jerry thought. *Am I really that tired and haggard looking? Or am I just no longer the carefree devil-may-care twenty-year-old that I had been?*

I'm not sure the mirror would have told Jerry the truth.

I've learned that cameras may tell us how others see us, but mirrors only reflect what our minds allow us to perceive.

Karen perceives the effects of gravity.

"When you go to the mirror, you suck in your cheekbones and try to lift everything up," she says. "You also look for firming action creams everywhere you go."

She recently bought a new one with seaweed that promises miracle skin lifting.

"You put it on your face, and you can't move," Karen said, "but you look good for a while."

Whatever works—even for just a couple hours.

After all, as they say . . . it hurts to be beautiful.

Gray hair is a crown of splendor; it is attained by a righteous life.

PROVERBS 16:31

nine

The Eyes Have Had It

And the ears aren't
doing too great either.

It is only with the heart that one can see rightly;
What is essential is invisible to the eye.

ANTOINE DE SAINT-EXUPERY

Now you see it; now you don't.

What was once a slogan is now a fact of life.

As you get older, your eyesight starts to go. At least that's what all my friends and family tell me.

I can't personally vouch for that as I've always had perfect vision and can read signs two miles away, as well as the fine print on candy wrappers from across the room.

Not so for my sister, Lisa, who has worn glasses—or contacts—since grade school.

"Last year I decided to appease my vain self and go get contacts again," she said. "Because I need bifocals now, the doctor tried to use a contact for distance vision in one eye and near vision in the other. Instead of seeing clearly, I had to close one eye to see anything while I drove. My eye muscles aren't what they used to be, so I would get tired and open the closed eye.

"Then I was really in trouble," Lisa said.

"Back to the doctor I went. He gave me two contacts for distance vision and told me to get 'readers' (little half glasses) and wear those when I read."

In Lisa's line of work—a teacher in a medical trade college—she's always reading.

And since reading is her favorite hobby at home, she was wearing her little half glasses all the time. "Unless of course I wanted to see things in the distance," she said. "The 'readers' made everything blurry, so I had to pull them down my nose and look *over* them."

One day at school Lisa was standing at the podium lecturing when one of her students looked at her and yelled out, "Hey, Miss Cook; you know who you look like with those little glasses? Granny Goose."

"That did it," Lisa said. "I certainly don't want to look like a granny, much less a goose!" She popped out her contacts that night and went back to wearing glasses.

Our cousin Kathy also had to invest in a pair of reading glasses.

"I was reading the newspaper one day, and it was odd that I had to hold the paper up a little higher to see it," she recalled.

"My husband looked at me strangely and asked, 'Is there a reason you have your glasses on upside down?'"

Although Nurse Karen's sister wore her brand-new bifocals right side up, they made her nauseous.

"The hardest thing for her was getting up the stairs," said Karen, sympathetically. "She didn't know whether to look over the line or under."

Bifocals aren't the only lines to be considered.

In addition to the laugh lines on either side of her eyes, Karen's also noticed her eyelids are beginning to droop.

"As they start to droop, you lose your peripheral vision," she explained. "That's why people have their eyelids lifted."

The good news is insurance will pay for an eyelift. The bad news is only if you lose your vision due to it.

What about my lost emotional well-being?

If insurance covers counseling, why not an eyelift? It would make me feel much happier—and be so much cheaper than those weekly therapy sessions.

I think my friend Jan might be able to get one of those insurance-paid eyelifts.

"As usual these days, I totally forgot to refill my monthly medication," she said. "So I checked the bottle and dialed the pharmacy number. Much to my surprise, I heard an automated voice say, 'The number you have dialed has been disconnected and there is no other number.'

"My neck stiffened, and my heart leaped," Jan recalled. "What? How can this be?

The good news is insurance will pay for an eyelift. The bad news is only if you lose your vision due to it.

"I checked the label again. Yes, that was the number—4225667.

"'Carl,' I shouted to my husband, 'the drugstore must have gone out of business and never told us.'"

Carl took the bottle from his wife, dialed the number, and reached a pharmacist happy to accommodate his request.

"After he hung up," Jan said, "he smiled at me and said, 'You dialed the prescription number.'"

At least Jan only dialed a wrong number.

My aunt Char once mistook some antibiotic salve for her toothpaste.

I'm thankful I don't have any eye problems . . . yet.

But my ears are another thing altogether.

The older I get, the less I can tolerate noise.

That's why I always try to grab the remote first when we're going to watch a movie.

My delicate eardrums simply can't stand that horrible loud static noise that comes when you first switch over from TV to VCR.

Before the videotape has even finished popping into the VCR, I immediately hit the mute button. That way I don't have to hear even a millisecond of static.

I always mute commercials too. Talk about annoyingly loud noise.

Only problem is, I've been left out in the cultural cold on more than one occasion. "Hey, have you seen the commercial with the cute talking dog who says . . ."

Well, yes, I've *seen* it; just never *heard* it.

The only dog I ever hear is our adowable widdle canine daughter, Gracie.

Her mommy wearly, wearly wuvs her good widdle girl, but sometimes—just sometimes, Mommy's good girl barks just a widdle too much for Mommy's noise-level tolerance.

That's when Gracie gets sent to "exile" (Michael's craft studio—which also doubles as the guest room, complete with comfortable bed).

Used to be, I had to carry her into exile.

Now I just point and say the word.

Gracie trots straight into the studio, hops onto the end of the bed, curls up, and patiently waits to be released.

If only words worked as well for me.

As I get older, I'm having a little difficulty finding just the right words to say—which can spell real trouble for a writer.

Thankfully, it's just a vocal problem.

Recently, after about nine or ten straight hours of writing, I was pretty fried—as was my computer.

As I wearily closed the now-warm laptop, I said, "Time to give this computer a breast."

Can you say way tired?

I meant to say *break*, or *rest*.

My friend Karen meant to say *glad* or *happy*, but what came out was, "I'm so glappy!"

She has such a way with words—the wrong words.

There was the time Karen was having breakfast in New York with a good friend when she leaned over to her friend and graciously asked, "Would you like some more syrup on your pajamas?"

Translation: pancakes.

Much later that day she said, "M'mmm, this is really good camera."

Translation: candy.

"That's what you call being on the wrong page of the Rolodex," she explains.

In Michael's case, it was the wrong side of the cubicle.

One day at work, he heard one of his female coworkers say, "I'm in a pothole."

Bemused, because the last time he checked, there were no potholes in the office carpet, he walked over to her cubicle.

"I'm menopausal," was what she'd said.

That day Michael decided to get both his hearing and his eyes checked.

During his visit to the eye doctor, a nurse put in some drops to dilate his eyes and told him he could drive, but he had to wear sunglasses to protect his eyes from light.

On the way home, he stopped at the grocery store to buy me something for dinner—still wearing his sunglasses since his eyes were light sensitive. Other shoppers looked at him curiously, trying to figure out if he was a movie star or a punk rocker.

Once home, Michael came in the kitchen to kiss me hello—still wearing the sunglasses.

He pulled a package out of the grocery bag and handed it to me with a flourish: "Here, honey, I bought you some liver since you haven't had any in a while and you need your iron."

Talk about true love.

Michael HATES liver—the taste, sight, smell—the very *thought* of it turns his stomach.

But he went out of his way to buy me some since he knows how much I like it, and more importantly, that I need it since I tend to be slightly anemic.

Only problem was . . . it was beef *heart.*

With his eyes dilated and the sunglasses on, he couldn't read the writing on the package, and since he's not an internal organ man, one vital organ looked pretty much like another.

I was very touched by his heartfelt gesture—but not enough to eat heart.

> *"My grace is sufficient for you, for my power is made perfect in weakness."*
>
> 2 CORINTHIANS 12:9

ten

Food for Thought

My tastebuds may still be young,
but my stomach's not what it used to be.

I wish my ulcers and I could get together on a mutually satisfactory diet.

IRVIN S. COBB

In my twenties, the only thing that gave me heartburn was men.

Now, in my forties, everything does.

Steak, lobster, cheeseburgers. (All except Big Macs for some reason.)

Even Miracle Whip.

Rats. There go my tuna fish sandwiches.

Problem is, I have the tastebuds of a twenty-year-old but the stomach of a seventy-year-old.

It's called acid reflux.

Most people take Tums, Rolaids, or some other antacid for this midlife-and-more problem.

Not me.

I have my own home remedy that works really well.

Here's what you do:

You take a great big bite of a greasy bacon cheeseburger or a steak dripping with butter and salt, chew just four or five times, and then while this yummy, artery-clogging red meat is still making its fattening way down to your stomach, you suddenly start beating the center of your chest with your fist while simultaneously expelling fast puffs of breath from your mouth.

Michael calls it my Tarzan act.

But it's really more like Tarzan-Lamaze.

Caution: The Tarzan-Lamaze act works best at home. Performing it in public isn't very ladylike. Besides, in a restaurant, you're apt to encounter an overly solicitous waiter just itching to perform the Heimlich maneuver.

Therefore, in the interest of embarrassing-dining-heroics prevention and polite society, I've come up with a kinder, gentler version.

Ladylike-renditon of the Tarzan-Lamaze act:

Take a smaller bite of a greasy bacon cheeseburger or a steak dripping with butter and salt, chew six or seven times, and then while this yummy, artery-clogging red meat is still making its fattening way down to your genteel stomach, start unobtrusively patting the center of your bosom with your open palm—gently, oh-so gently—while simultaneously expelling quiet, slower puffs of breath from your mouth.

If you do it discreetly enough, people will think you're having a hot flash.

Otherwise, just order chicken.

I've become the queen of chicken.

Baked chicken, broiled chicken, grilled chicken, rotisserie chicken, chicken and rice, chicken and noodles, chicken-and-broccoli casserole, chicken a la king, chicken surprise . . .

Chicken is the best friend of the heartburn impaired.

Closely followed by turkey.

But I have to tell you, this girl—who's always liked a little spice in her life: chili, enchiladas, chimichangas, chips and salsa, lasagna, and curry—is getting pretty bored with poultry.

Don't get me wrong.

I adore turkey at Thanksgiving—hand over that drumstick!—and turkey sandwiches afterwards, but enough is enough.

Last year, we had Thanksgiving at my mom's and with our big crowd, there wasn't much turkey remaining for leftovers, so Michael went out the next day and bought our own—an eighteen-pounder.

The following week, we repeated Thanksgiving dinner at our house, inviting a friend to join us for the feast.

It was delicious. Nothing in the world like turkey, stuffing, mashed potatoes, and gravy—all homemade.

And for Michael, peas.

He loves peas with his mashed potatoes and gravy. For him, it's just not Thanksgiving without peas—which has created some pretty funny misunderstandings at our family holiday table. First, it was my sister who thought Michael said he liked "creamed peas" (for the whole saga, which I won't belabor here, read *Love Handles for the Romantically Impaired*) and then this year, my mom thought it was peas and pearl onions.

But it's just plain old peas. It's the *combination* of peas, mashed potatoes, and gravy that's nirvana to him.

You'll never catch me using peas and nirvana in the same sentence. I *hate* peas: plain, creamed, or with pearl onions.

It's a texture thing.

Oops. Sorry. Went off on a little pea tangent there.

Anyway, the day after our second Thanksgiving dinner, I had a turkey sandwich for lunch. And for dinner that night we had leftover turkey, stuffing, mashed potatoes, and gravy, peas for Michael, and green beans for me.

But the next night when my honey came home from work and wanted Thanksgiving leftovers yet again, I opted for a burrito instead.

Michael went for the big bird.

Not me. My tastebuds were in full turkey revolt.

Can you say bored out of my mouth?

By that point, a little heartburn was preferable to any more tastebud monotony. And since we were home, I knew it was safe to let loose with my full-on Tarzan-Lamaze act, even adding in a couple burps for good measure. (Not to worry, the burps are for Michael's and Gracie's ears only.)

Many of my middle-aged friends suffer from heartburn, including Lonnie.

"I can't eat two hours before I go to sleep due to acid reflux," she says, "and definitely no tomatoes or fried food at night."

Lonnie travels a lot with her work. One evening in Nashville, Tennessee, she had dinner with some colleagues at a restaurant that served deep-fried frog legs. They were very tasty—until about midnight. The heartburn woke her out of a sound sleep.

She called the hotel desk to see if they had any antacids. This was a small hotel without room service or much in their vending machines. The young man at the desk drawled very kindly, "I find a nice glass of Sprite helps at a time like this." And within minutes, he brought Sprite to her room, at no charge.

"It was sweet of him," she says, "though it didn't do me much good."

Now Lonnie always packs Tums in her suitcase.

And she thinks frog legs look a whole lot better on frogs.

Hmmmm, I think the time has come for me to teach her the Tarzan-Lamaze act—just in case she runs out of Tums.

From the fruit of his mouth a man's stomach is filled;
with the harvest from his lips he is satisfied.
PROVERBS 18:20

eleven

Let's Hear It for All the Fuddy-Duddies!

Just when did I become one?

Few people know how to be old.

FRANCOIS, DUC DE LA ROCHEFOUCALD

I've become a fuddy-duddy.

It's an age thing.

Years ago, in my twenties, I found it necessary to always be going somewhere, doing something, or trying some new adventure.

That's why I joined the Air Force after high school; I was looking for some excitement off in that wild blue yonder.

And I thought that people who weren't like me were boring.

In fact, I used to always call my friends Pat and Ken—who are just a decade older than I am—fuddy-duddies because they liked to stay home a lot.

How dull is that?

To me, a single woman living in Europe and always on the go, their lives seemed uneventful and mundane.

I didn't realize there was a difference between dull and content.

Now my twenty-three-year-old nephew considers *me* a fuddy-duddy.

Only I think he uses a different word.

Boring with a capital B.

He finds it hard to believe that Michael and I don't stay up to welcome in the New Year (I think in nearly ten years of marriage, we've only managed to stay up until midnight once).

Josh—and his mom—were sure we'd stay up to usher in the new millennium.

And we tried. Really we did.

I think we made it all the way to 11:30, but by then our eyelids were drooping big-time, so we did something that was really exciting for us instead.

Went to sleep.

That qualifies as major fuddy-duddydom.

So do naps.

I love naps.

Remember those happy rainbow days of kindergarten where each afternoon you and all your kinder-friends got to pull out your little red mats and lay on the floor for mandatory snooze time?

Although, come to think of it, when I was in kindergarten I never wanted to nap—I always wanted to play or read instead.

What really surprised me was that my mom took naps every day—something I never understood as a child. I mean, she was a grown-up! She could do what she wanted—no one was *making* her take a nap.

Now that I'm in my forties, I finally "get" the nap thing and am proudly following in Mom's curled-up-on-the-couch footsteps at least once or twice a week.

If I don't get my Sunday nap, look out.

But I'm not quite as bad as my friend Katie.

She's only a year older than I am, but if she doesn't get her daily nap, she's not happy.

And if Katie ain't happy, ain't nobody happy.

Another way I've joined the fuddy-duddy or old-fogy brigade is my distaste for crowds. Jostling hordes of people make me crazy—and just a teensy bit claustrophobic.

Yet when I was younger, I loved to go to crowded parties and dance clubs.

Of course, I used to think I was a "city girl" too—until I went to five major cities on a book tour last year, beginning with the Big Apple.

Ever since I was a little girl, I dreamed of going to New York: Broadway, Times Square, Radio City Music Hall, the hustle and bustle of the subway, yellow cabs crowding the streets . . .

Some of it was incredibly exciting and memorable: going to the top of the Empire State Building—although not finding either Cary Grant or Tom Hanks up there—seeing *Les Miserables* on Broadway, and going to the Carnegie Deli for a skyscraper slice of New York cheesecake.

But by the fourth day, those busy city sidewalks, rushing, honking taxicabs, and all that concrete were just a little too much for this Sacramento girl. (Although Sacramento is the capital of California, it's not as big and cosmopolitan as say . . . Los Angeles or San Francisco—thankfully.)

From the Big Apple we went to Chicago, Atlanta, Dallas, and L.A.

Beverly Hills, that is. Swimming pools. Movie stars.

Although I didn't see one swimming pool or movie star.

But I did see a lot of thin, beautiful women in tight leather pants that could have been movie stars. (Can you imagine having a hot flash in leather?)

There's a law in Beverly Hills that says women there can't weigh more than 110.

If they do, the streets will buckle and crack.

I really took my life in my hands by walking to a nearby restaurant with Michael for dinner. We had a couple close calls but made it safely back to the hotel with only a couple minor cracks in the pavement.

On the way we passed by stores with names like Tiffany's, Saks, and Barney's of New York.

The only Barney I know is big and purple and sings an annoyingly repetitive song.

Can you say fish out of water?

There's a law in Beverly Hills
that says women there
can't weigh more than 110.

I am so NOT a California girl. Most people—who don't live in California—envision these bronzed, blonde, Baywatch beauties populating the streets and beaches of the Golden State.

I'm neither bronzed nor blonde, and I don't run in slow motion on the beach—or anywhere actually.

In fact, I'm two hours away from the nearest beach.

So the best thing about Beverly Hills to me was . . . (hold on, major fuddy-duddy response coming up) the number of TV channels.

See, we don't have cable at home, and by this point on the tour, I needed as much "veg time" as I could get.

So, while Michael headed to the nearest museum, I killed three hours before my first media interview by switching back and forth between all the old movie channels I could find.

It was great.

I got to see *No Time for Sergeants* with Andy Griffith and the first half of an old Ginger Rogers movie.

That's when I knew I was really a suburbs girl.

Shopping malls confirmed it.

Although we have a mega mall in Sacramento with more than a hundred stores, the gentler, kinder local twenty-store mall just four blocks away is more my style.

Even in our not-so-big city, my crowd distaste has reared its fuddy-duddy head.

Last summer, for the first time in years, Michael and I went to the State Fair. We went the first year we were married, but I got sick on the Ferris wheel—a combined effect of the corn dogs, cotton candy, and crowd—so we skipped it the following couple years.

This time, I was ready to leave when we got to the entrance.

It's a long, hot walk all the way from that big old parking lot.

However, we stayed for almost two hours, without riding one ride. We sure did see lots of fascinating exhibits though—the true sign of a fuddy-duddy.

And on the Fourth of July, rather than going out to watch the fireworks, we popped in *To Catch a Thief* with Cary Grant and Grace Kelly instead. There's that one really great fireworks scene, you know.

But nothing can make you feel like an old fogy faster than being around a bunch of twenty-year-olds.

My first week on a brand-new job, I joined my youngish coworkers for lunch in the break room.

Now I've always been a pretty outgoing person—able to talk to anyone about anything. But on this day I felt like a stranger in a strange land.

My coworkers—all in their early twenties—were talking about *South Park* (never seen it), *The Simpsons* (missed that too), Counting Crows, Red Hot Chili Peppers, and Nine-Inch Nails.

107

Well, I'd heard of eating crow, not counting them; red-hot chili peppers give me indigestion, and it seems to me that nine-inch nails would have to be used for some pretty big building projects—nothing we'd tackle around the house.

Finally it dawned on me that they were talking about popular bands.

That's when the generation gap smacked me right in the face.

Talk about feeling white bread and old.

If it hadn't been for the one twenty-three-year-old guy who shared my love of Sinatra, I'd have been toast.

But when they started talking about weekend parties that lasted until 3:00 A.M., I knew I'd really bit the old-age dust.

Other than our annual Academy Awards intimate soiree, the only parties I go to these days involve candles, kitchen gadgets, or Tupperware.

And they're always over by 10:00 P.M.

You know you're in full fuddy-duddyhood when plastic is a party.

Live now, believe me, wait not till tomorrow; gather the roses of life today.

PIERRE DE RONSARD

twelve

The Middle-Age Top 40 Chart

A scientific, important list no woman over forty
should ever be without.

Old people like to give good advice, as solace for no longer being able to provide bad examples.

FRANCOIS, DUC DE LA ROCHEFOUCALD

Okay, now that you've reached middle age, it's important that you be able to identify all those exciting physical and mental changes you're going through.

That's why I've taken the time, dear reader, to compile this very scientific, thoroughly researched, and exhaustive list for you. Although, you might want to write it down so you don't forget it.

Very Scientific and Exhaustive List of Middle-Age Terms

1. Age Spots	Cute freckles gone bad.
2. Arm Flaps	Those under-the-upper-arm swings that can knock out a man, woman, or child from across the room. (First spotted on the scary flying monkeys in *The Wizard of Oz*.)
3. Bifocals	What you wear so you can see all your brand-new facial hair. (Caution: May cause dizziness.)
4. Brain Fade	What mine is doing right now as I try to finish this book at 3:30 A.M.
5. Chin Hair	A continuous thread of conclusive aging (and yet another new place to pluck).

6. Crow's Feet	The tracks of my tears; whatever happened to that spring chicken?
7. Double Chin	The ultimate in rubber necking.
8. Dropped Derriere	When you can see your backside from the front.
9. The Drop Zone	The area of the body—from the eyelids to the kneecaps—where everything starts to go south for the winter . . . spring . . . summer.
10. Eye Lift	Expensive surgical procedure to give you that taut, youthful wide-eyed look instead of Dean Martin's droop.
11. Fan	Essential weapon in the hot-flash war. No menopausal woman should ever leave home without it.
12. Fuddy-Duddy	You've turned into a fuddy-duddy when the only party you go to is Tupperware.
13. Gingko	Miracle supplement to help you remember why you opened the door of the refrigerator.
14. Gray Hair	On men it may look distinguished, but for women, it's something we try to extinguish.
15. HRT	(Hormone Replacement Therapy) AKA Hot Flash First Aid.
16. Hot Flash	Better than an I.D., this furnace blast from the waist up tells everyone around you that you're over forty.

17. Law of Forgetfulness	If it isn't written down, you'll forget it.
18. Menopause	The only time in your life you get to have the same wardrobe from season to season—all summer clothes (which means white after Labor Day, Mom).
19. Menopausal Mustache	Something every woman over forty can look forward to bleaching, plucking, or waxing.
20. Mentalpause	Inability to remember names, places, and what you were just about to say (AKA brain fade, or senior moment).
21. Middle Age	Caught between a glamour girl and a golden girl.
22. Middle-Age Spread	A tummy just waiting to be tucked.
23. Midlife Crisis	When your husband comes home one day astride a Harley or sporting a pierced eyebrow.
24. Mood Swings	Pick a mood, any mood, then change it in a heartbeat, add tears, and stir.
25. Mother-in-the-Mirror	Mirror, mirror on the wall. Instead of looking like Snow White, you're your mother after all.
26. Naps	Ecstasy.
27. Night Sweats	A good reason to shop the white sales.

28. Pencil Test	Important perky teen coming-of-age ritual along with SATs. After forty, do NOT attempt at home.
29. Perimenopause	The beginning of the end.
30. PMS	A walk in the park next to menopause.
31. Puffy Thighs	Forget cottage cheese thighs, we're talking mega-marshmallows here.
32. Reading Glasses	Also known as cheaters, now available at your local drugstore for only ten bucks.
33. Sex after Fifty	Huh? Did you say something, dear?
34. Thermostat Wars	He may get the remote, but you've won the real battle: supreme control of the thermostat.
35. Thinning Hair	A wig a day keeps the bald spot at bay.
36. Varicose Veins	Coast-to-coast road map permanently imprinted on your legs, complete with rivers, mountains, and railroad tracks.
37. Vitamins	What you have to take in order to keep having sex after fifty.
38. Warm Wave	Baby hot flash.
39. Whatchamacallit	Latest word addition to the middle-age dictionary—must be said in tandem with pointing at common, everyday object.

40. Wrinkle Cream   Save your money. Buy chocolate
                         instead.

He who began a good work in you will carry it on to completion until the day of Christ Jesus.

PHILIPPIANS 1:6

thirteen

His Mid-Yikes Crisis

Women have hormonal ups and downs,
but men buy motorcycles.

I've always believed in the adage that the secret of eternal youth is arrested development.

ALICE ROOSEVELT LONGWORTH

I think Alice Roosevelt Longworth knew what she was talking about when it came to eternal youthfulness. After all, she was the daughter of Theodore Roosevelt, the active, adventurous, and, at age forty-two, youngest president of the United States.

Teddy Roosevelt, commander of the Rough Riders cavalry unit, conservationist, trustbuster, Nobel Peace Prize winner, and big game hunter, was well noted for his spirit of adventure and active life.

Not a man you'd expect to see sitting in a rocking chair.

My husband has always admired Teddy Roosevelt. In fact, as an actor, he'd like to portray him someday.

Actually, the role he'd really like to play is Teddy Brewster in *Arsenic and Old Lace.* That Teddy just *thinks* he's Theodore Roosevelt and spends his time digging in the basement for locks for the Panama Canal, or drawing out his pretend sword and yelling "Cha-a-a-a-rge" as he runs up the stairs in what he thinks is his famous attack on San Juan Hill.

Teddy Brewster was definitely acting out a midlife crisis.

Not all men go to such extremes.

After my brother-in-law Jim turned fifty, he pierced his ear.

It was the cheapest midlife crisis he could think of.

Besides, if Harrison Ford could do it, why not Jim?

When I was officially diagnosed as being perimenopausal, Michael took it in stride. After all, we had sort of been expecting it because of the aftereffects of chemotherapy.

119

He was probably relieved that my erratic behavior was due to something scientific.

He's such a guy.

Then he realized, "I'm still in my thirties (barely), and my wife is going through The Change!"

That's when he started *planning* his midlife crisis.

"Since things happen to us early, I thought I'd get a jump start on this too," he said.

Trouble was, he couldn't decide what to do.

He can't afford the red convertible or the cabin in the mountains, doesn't want a motorcycle or girlfriend—good thing—and is too practical to change careers at this point in his life.

Now, have you ever heard of someone logically planning a midlife crisis?

That's my honey.

I've even caught him e-mailing high school friends— collaborating on a strategy.

He decided he wanted to learn oil painting, so I bought him a set of paints, brushes, and a few blank canvases for his birthday.

But since that birthday weekend, he hasn't picked up a brush.

"Someday soon," he keeps saying.

My best friend's husband's midlife crisis involved buy- ing a snazzy new car.

Although, actually, come to think of it, the car was really more his wife's midlife crisis since she'd just turned forty.

"We saw the BMW Z-3 in a James Bond movie and fell in love with it," said Lana, drooling. "We really wanted to get it, but it was a tad too small, so practicality took over."

Instead, they got a shiny black BMW 323 four-door sporty sedan.

Car changes seem to be a midlife theme.

Jim and Judi Braddy recently bought their first convertible.

"It's a shiny red LeBaron LSL with power everything," Judi said excitedly.

"It's mostly been a fantasy the last few years—the idea of driving a convertible, even a joke at times between Jim and me," she said, "sort of like the Harley he's going to buy someday. A big one that we can just jump on and go wherever and whenever we feel like—without room for a lot of baggage to weigh us down."

Although the Braddys joked about the convertible, lately, more and more Judi found herself looking at every one that passed them on the road.

"I would always try to catch a glimpse of the driver—just to see if I fit the image," she said. "What I discovered was that convertible drivers come in all shapes, sizes, and ages—but a lot of them looked my age and older.

"Maybe that was part of my problem. I guess at forty-six—pushing forty-seven—driving a convertible seemed to me a little too closely connected with a midlife crisis."

But upon test driving the shiny red LeBaron, Judi quickly got over her qualms.

"With the top down but windows rolled up, I pulled cautiously out of the car lot and turned the corner," she recalled. "The light turned green and as we picked up a little speed, I decided to throw caution to the wind and roll down all the windows."

Once that warm California breeze began blowing through her hair, Judi was hooked.

Although she and Jim have another car—a company car—they always find themselves looking now for opportunities to drive the convertible.

Mary and Charlie—who are in their fifties—have a snazzy red convertible too: a Miata with the license plate 1FRESOL (Charlie's Blazer is FRESOL2).

H'mmmm, I wonder if Michael and I will want a convertible when we get to our fifties. Personally, I'd settle for a garbage disposal.

My uncle Jimmy never got a convertible, but he definitely encountered a midlife crisis when he retired.

After surviving colon cancer and a heart bypass, he went into a blue funk for a while just hanging around the house with nothing to do—except plan trips he wanted to take.

My aunt Sharon would come home from work to find a slew of travel books and maps for whatever place had caught his fancy that day. Happily, she has since retired too, and now they're taking fun trips together—including visits to us in California.

Ken never went through a midlife crisis.

"I'm pretty realistic about getting older," he said contentedly. "I've got my mate for life, we travel, I enjoy my home, my life . . . what am I going to do?"

He could always try karaoke.

Midlife crises are not the only signs of male aging.

Over the years, Dan Mouw had gotten very bad at noticing when his wife Bonnie gets her hair cut.

"After one haircut—I had several inches cut off—he never noticed," Bonnie recalled.

"Finally, after two weeks, we were both standing in front of the mirror one evening. He was behind me, so I began fussing with my hair in a rather exaggerated way—all the while watching his face in the mirror.

"It took a little bit of time, but finally he looked at my hair. His whole countenance changed.

"I could see the wheels turning. I was sure I could read his thoughts: *Oh, dear. She got her hair cut. Was it today? A few days ago? Should I say something? If I do and it's been awhile, I'm in trouble. If I don't and it was today, I'm in trouble.*

"Finally he said, 'You got your hair cut! It looks nice.'

"We had a good laugh when I told him it had been two weeks."

But the experience sharpened him up. The next time Bonnie told him she had an appointment to get a haircut, he wrote it down in his book.

Unfortunately for him, she had to reschedule the appointment.

That night when he got home from work, he looked at his wife and said, "You got your hair cut. I like it!"

"You should have seen the look on his face when I told him that I'd rescheduled the appointment for the following day," Bonnie recalled with a giggle.

"The next day I had my hair cut at 1:00 P.M. and went back to work. At about 2:00 P.M., I got a phone call from my husband who said, 'I love your haircut!'"

The haircut-noticing Dan is also a private pilot.

His midlife crisis has been worse than most men's.

"He went through just about every stage you hear about," said Bonnie.

"The red convertible stage, the permed hair stage, the black Camaro T-top stage, and the 'cool clothes' stage—but unfortunately it hasn't stopped there.

"I tell women to count their blessings if all their husbands do is buy flashy cars.

"Now my husband wants to buy an airplane."

Oh, by the way, Michael finally decided what to do for his midlife crisis: go to Disneyland—again.

Michael finally decided what to do for his midlife crisis: go to Disneyland—again.

A man may grow old in body, but never in mind.

CICERO

fourteen

Not in the Mood

For Scrabble, Spades, or any bedroom games
that start with "S."

An archaeologist is the best husband a woman can have;
the older she gets, the more interested he is in her.

AGATHA CHRISTIE

My friend Karen says that menopause is a pause from men: Get AWAY from me!

Trisha says it's not that she wants her husband to get away, it just takes a lot longer to get going.

"It seems strange to me that when we are young and have ravenous sex drives, our lives are full of kids and work and houses and on and on," she says.

"We look forward to the day when we can make love without all the distractions, but then when that day comes, voila, the sex drive has gone underground. I know it's in there somewhere; just give me an hour or two and I'll find it.

"Isn't that just a bit backward? Now we have a whole evening together, no kids, no noise—a situation I would have killed for earlier.

"But then, it's good that we've got all evening, because that's what it takes to get the old fire burning."

Or as Henri Estienne so eloquently put it: "If youth but knew, if old age but could."

Another friend of mine—who prefers to remain anonymous—told the story of her sixty-eight-year-old husband, "Jack," a prostate cancer survivor.

Now Jack's a pretty frugal guy. So the first time he went to the drugstore after his prostate surgery—to fill his prescription for Viagra—he grumbled to his wife, "Never thought I'd pay for sex."

Prior to his surgery, when Jack was doing some research about his cancer, he read about the older couple who decided that rather than spending several thousand dollars for treatments or devices to solve the after-surgery sex problem, they'd remodel their kitchen instead.

Guess that was one time when the way to a man's heart was really through his stomach.

I've needed a remodeled kitchen for years . . .

But, for some reason, Michael's not about to exchange sex in favor of new countertops, a garbage disposal, and a built-in dishwasher.

What *is* it with men and sex anyway?

Doesn't he understand that if we *had* a built-in dishwasher, I'd spend less time in the kitchen and more in the bedroom?

Speaking of the bedroom . . .

One evening not long ago, Michael and I were snuggled on the couch watching a movie when a character actor who looked really familiar came on-screen.

"Honey, where have we seen him before?" I asked, trying to place the actor.

"He was the scientist in *Terminator 2*," Michael replied instantly.

"No, that's not it. That was a different guy," I said.

"No, dear," Michael sweetly contradicted me.

"Sorry, darling, you're mistaken," replied the confident Silver Screen Trivial Pursuit Queen. "In fact, I'll bet you four nights of lovemaking in a row that you're wrong."

Michael took that bet in a New York minute.

"But, honey, if you win, what do you get?" he asked, puzzled.

"NO sex for four nights in a row."

Michael won. (My mistake was that I failed to remember that he knows *Terminator 2* inside out—he even went to see it with a bunch of guys for his bachelor party.)

I never made a bet like that again.

Time definitely changes things—libido-wise.

A friend sent me this great quote she received over the Internet: "Old is when your sweetie says, 'Let's go upstairs and make love,' and you answer, 'Honey, I can't do both.'"

My friend Judi says that sexual intimacy has been an important and treasured part of her thirty-three years of married life.

"Raised with religious conviction in a generation that emphasized virginity prior to marriage, we waited for each other," she said. "And, oh baby, it was worth it! Over the years we've definitely made up for lost time.

"That's not to say there haven't been a few little intimate glitches due to stresses in different stages of our lives," Judi adds, "but we have learned two things that, I believe, have become especially important at this stage of the game.

1. Quality is better than quantity.
2. Timing is everything.

"In other words, sometimes it takes longer to get where we're going, but it's worth the journey. And sometimes the journey is pleasure enough even if we don't reach our destination," she declares.

Awake, north wind,
and come, south wind!
Blow on my garden,
that its fragrance may spread abroad.
Let my lover come into his garden
and taste its choice fruits.
Song of Songs 4:16

NOTE TO READER: You've probably noticed that this chapter is a little shorter than the rest . . . that's because it's about sex. And since the sex drive diminishes a bit in midlife anyway . . . I also thought my publisher might get a little uncomfortable with too much sex in this book, so I exercised a little discretion—much to my husband's relief. He's not that comfortable talking about sex to the whole world. He's more of an action kind of guy. In fact, even as I write this, Michael's come up behind me to whisper in my ear that he's just found a great buy on a new built-in dishwasher.

fifteen

Cry Me a River

Better step back from the waterworks that threaten
to explode at the slightest provocation.

Old age ain't no place for sissies.
BETTE DAVIS

During menopause, one destination many women seem to reach with increasing frequency is the valley of tears.

Also known as hormonal mood swings, the slightest little thing can set us off. Okay, ladies, all together now, join me in the mood swing cheer:

Swing to the left,
Swing to the right,
C'mon, mood swings,
Fight, cry, fight!

"A coworker simply said 'good morning' to me, and I burst into tears," said Karen. "I just started wailing."

"The most miserable thing about menopause is having the tears come on an instant's notice . . . about *any*thing!" says Jean Griswold. "Why does my husband feel like he has to tiptoe around me? And when our primary care physician asks him if the diet pills she's giving me are making me ornery, he replies, 'No more so than usual.'"

Sheri Jameson, my oh-so-sensible sister-in-law, recounted bewilderedly that recently her lunch just didn't taste right, so she started crying.

And Sheri's never been much of a crier.

Blame it on the menopause.

Peggy Clark cried at something a little more reasonable—technology.

"I always feel so inept at technical things anyway," she says. "And with my self-confidence sometimes taking a dip because I am definitely not getting any younger or growing any new brain cells, trying to master this new cell phone without feeling like a complete idiot seemed quite a task.

"My husband tried to be patient with me in taking me step-by-step through it when I only wanted to know how to dial a number, put it through, and wait for 'hello' on the other end. That's all.

"Not too much to ask. Right?

"Well, you see, this cell phone won't *just* do that," she explains. "It will send and receive mail, leave and receive voice mail, keep track of minutes left on my phone plan, store names and phone numbers, and get my attention when someone is calling by playing *Mozart's Concerto in B Flat*.

"Okay," she admits, "maybe that's not it but something similar—a classical piece anyway in digital sound. I had fifteen different beeps, tones, and songs to choose from.

"That's another toughie for me these days—making decisions. But that's another story . . ."

Frustrated by her inability to understand the ins and outs of the cell phone, Peggy wound up getting all choked up and emotional.

"I feel so stupid," she wailed to her practical-but-now-bemused husband. "Just tell me how the thing works. Don't ask me something like 'What do you think you should do next?'

"I hate that," she says now when recalling the incident. "It means I have to come up with the right answer, and I don't even understand the question."

I'm with Peggy.

Michael does that to me too.

It must be a guy thing.

He's convinced that if I "really applied myself" and wanted to understand technical or mechanical things, I could.

I remind him that when I took the Air Force proficiency exam twenty-five years ago, I scored in the nineties in administrative and general knowledge but got a whopping fifteen in mechanical.

My score certainly hasn't improved over the years. If anything, I'm sure it's diminished.

My brain just isn't wired for logic.

Or numbers.

I still count on my fingers, okay?

And even when I use a calculator, I can never get the numbers to add up to the same total twice in a row.

That's why I'm a writer rather than an accountant.

Or a computer programmer.

My brain just isn't wired for logic.

My twenty-three-year-old nephew Josh is a computer whiz. He lives, breathes, and practically sleeps with the stuff—building computers from scratch and spending all his spare time surfing the Web or playing computer games.

I have a middle-aged confession to make: I've never played *one* computer game—unless you count Jeopardy online that one time—nor do I have any desire to do so. It's just not my thing.

To me, the computer is simply a valuable work tool: I write books and articles on it, communicate with friends and colleagues through e-mail, and read the entertainment news of the day, but that's about it.

I've never even logged on to e-Bay.

I'd much rather read a book any day.

Josh would rather surf the Web.

Guess that's what they call the generation gap.

But I digress.

When I got my first laptop—the one I'm using right now to write this book—Josh came over to set it up and program it for me.

As he did, he kept up a running commentary of what he was doing until my eyes started to glaze over and my head ached.

I just didn't understand most of what he was explaining to me.

He just couldn't understand how I couldn't understand basic computer logic.

Michael's never been able to understand how I can't understand *any* logic.

He began commiserating with Josh who was getting very frustrated with me.

I got frustrated with both of them until I was ready to burst into tears.

"All I need to know is how to get in Word and access my e-mail," I snapped. "No bells, no whistles, and no computer games. Is that too much to ask?"

Karen didn't think it was too much to ask her thirty-something female boss, who was having a hard time keeping up with Karen's mood swings, to look up menopause on the Internet.

"You need to research it," Karen said emphatically. "I have *every* symptom, and I'm not the only menopausal woman you'll have to deal with. Just the first.

"You might want to be prepared," she warned her.

Karen also happened to mention to her boss, "I think I should start taking medication."

Her boss replied, "Oh, I think that would be really good."

"What do you mean?" Karen snarled. "IS THERE A PROBLEM???"

Live in harmony with one another; be sympathetic, love as brothers, be compassionate and humble.

1 PETER 3:8

sixteen

Where Have All My Memories Gone?

Lost in space . . .
or gone with the wind.

Forgetting what is behind and straining toward what is ahead, I press on toward the goal to win the prize.
PHILIPPIANS 3:13–14

M emories . . . light the corners of my mind."

My friend Jan Coleman loves to sing in the shower.

"While scrubbing up with extra moisturizing soap, I can mentally call up lyrics from every song on the pop charts since I was ten," she says proudly.

"But I can't recall if I've washed my hair—all the proof is down the drain."

This lack of total recall is why my psychologist friend Ruth—who is in her early fifties—has come up with what she calls "The Law of Forgetfulness."

"If it isn't written down, it doesn't exist or won't happen," she says. "The corollary to this law, however, is that if you don't *look* at the day planner, store list, or whatever, it might as well not be written down.

"And heaven help us if we lose the day planner!"

If it isn't written down, it doesn't exist.

She recalls her most embarrassing incident of forgetfulness when she was working at a rural county mental health agency.

One week Ruth met a teenage client and her mother who'd come to the agency for help—during a week in which Ruth had several new clients (three of which involved fifteen-year-old girls and their single mothers).

The following week, the mother and teenage daughter returned.

"Their names were familiar," Ruth said, "but I wasn't sure if it was because I had seen them before or because I had looked at their names on the appointment roster." Medical Records neglected to give her the chart, which would have included her notes from the previous visit— "a very good clue that I had already seen them," she added.

"They looked vaguely familiar, but as I get older, I find that almost everyone looks vaguely familiar to me, so that was no help. Alas, I began the session asking them many of the elementary questions we had covered the previous week," Ruth said. "Finally the mother complained that she had to answer the same questions the last session; what was wrong with me that I couldn't remember what we talked about the previous week?

"I lamely excused myself by saying I had met three very similar families in rapid succession and that I had no chart to refer to," recalled Ruth. Meanwhile, she was asking herself, "How could I not remember these people from only a week before? They must think I'm an idiot!

"Well of course they thought I was an idiot, and they never came back," she said regretfully.

"That's when I realized how important written words are to my memory. With just a few glances at my notes, I can dazzle them with brilliance instead of baffling them with befuddlement. I just have to make sure I have the words in front of me."

I wish I'd known about Ruth's corollary earlier.

For my last book, *Thanks for the Mammogram!*, my publisher generously sent me on a book tour.

Part of the tour involved what's known as a morning radio drive blitz: I appear as a guest on one radio show after another—by phone from home—in rapid succession around the country to promote my book.

(An aside: Everyone thinks authors lead glamorous, exciting lives, and what could be more glamorous than a book tour? Actually I thought that too . . . before I went on my first tour. And I'm very grateful. Most of it was quite exciting—including my first stretch limo ride. But there's nothing very glamorous about waking up at 3:45 in the morning to prepare for a 4:00 A.M. [my West Coast time] interview [7:00 A.M. their East Coast time].)

So there I was, bleary-eyed, hair sticking out all over, clad in my Mickey Mouse nightshirt and Winnie-the-Pooh slippers, trying to cheerfully don my humor hat before the sun had even come up and gulping Earl Grey between interviews.

Good thing none of the stations had one of those new video phones.

By the thirteenth interview, I couldn't remember if I'd already told this particular radio host my funniest sound byte or sung "The Mammogram Song."

So by the final two interviews, I was saying to the hosts, "You'll have to forgive me; I'm going through mentalpause right now. Did I already tell you the one about . . . ?"

When Michael got home that night and I told him how I started to zone out on the air that morning, he suggested that I make up a list of my answers and sound bytes in advance. Then during each interview I would make a check mark next to each one as I say it.

"Thanks, honey. I'll be sure to remember that when I do my next morning radio drive blitz—*next* year."

I was happy to discover that forgetfulness even applies to college professors, as evidenced by my friend Maria Hunt.

"There's the one about forgetting the name of a person you just talked about in class, someone with a weird name like 'Phineas Gage.'

"The student asks you to 'spell that guy's name, the one with the spike through his head,' and you stand there panicking because you know whom they're talking about, but you're having to go through the alphabet to give you a clue.

"It's not A; could it start with B? No. How about C . . . ?

"You have to admit that you can't come up with his name, that it's one of the benefits of getting older—it takes more time for you to sort through your mental files. At least I *use* it as a learning experience," she chuckles.

"Then there's the class charades, or the 'sounds like' game I put students through when I forget something that's obvious. (I use the 'sounds like' symbol as I pinch my ear in my request for help.)

"Let's say I'm talking about a video we're creating in class," Maria says. "I can ask if the camera has been reserved, if the students have been called, if those 'THINGS' have been purchased. When the students look at me quizzically, I have to go through the phenomenon of, 'You know; you put it in the camera.'

"You put it in the camera to record the video . . .

"Most students have learned to enjoy these moments going through the guessing game with me. We'd see who would come up with the word first—*videotape*."

Jill, another teacher, recommends investing in a notepad or lots of sticky notes.

"You'll need them," she says. "I can't tell you how often I head off somewhere to get something, only to get there and not know why I went."

Isn't mentalpause maddening?

I think the time has come to invest in some gingko.

That's what Dan Mouw did.

"Dan was becoming concerned about his forgetfulness," his wife Bonnie said, "and he heard so much about the wonders of gingko that he bought some and began taking it faithfully. He was sure his memory was improving, but of course, it was a big secret—he didn't want anyone to know that he was taking such a thing.

"One Saturday evening, we were out on our usual date—eating out," she recalled. "We had run a few errands first, and then the plan was to go directly to the restaurant.

"Dan began heading in the wrong direction, so I asked him what was up.

"'I have to go home for a minute,' he said.

"I asked him why, and he hemmed and hawed a bit and finally said, 'I forgot something.'

"Of course, I couldn't let it go at that," said his curious wife, "so I pressed him to find out what it was.

"He replied sheepishly, 'I forgot to take my gingko!'"

I think Dan needs to take a hint from my friend Ruth and her Law of Forgetfulness.

Michael says I do too.

In the middle of writing this book, I was reading a chapter aloud to Michael for his feedback, and we both agreed that a specific sentence should be deleted.

I said I'd remember it later, but my beloved immediately sprang up to get a pen.

As he handed it to me, he said, "Don't trust the brain."

> *My son, do not forget my teaching, but keep my commands in your heart, for they will prolong your life many years.*
>
> PROVERBS 3:1–2

seventeen

From Sweet Nothings to Metamucil Murmurings

Ah, how the language of love
changes over the years.

When your friends begin to flatter you on how young you look, it's a sure sign you're getting old.

MARK TWAIN

It's late at night and the lights are turned down low; you lean over to romantically whisper sweet nothings in his ear, and instead you hear yourself saying,

"Dear, did you remember to take your Metamucil today?"

"Dear, did you remember to take your Metamucil today?"

Ah, the joys of aging.

Funny how those ardent murmurings between couples change over the years.

The big question among the middle-aged set now is to cruise or not to cruise.

Ken and Pat McLatchey are on the "not to cruise" side—portside, way off port.

They like to explore new, romantic—and luxurious— places off the beaten track. But on *their* timetable, not someone else's—so to them, being "stuck" on a cruise ship would be too confining and inhibiting.

To me, it would be paradise.

Plenty of time to read, relax, take it easy, read—while at the same time having the opportunity to visit new and exotic locales—and yet be back in time for the midnight buffet.

Cruising is just one of the favorite topics of choice among today's fiftysomethings . . . along with retirement, vitamins, fiber, and grandkids.

"The big T (travel) and the big R (retirement) are the two main topics of conversation," says Ken, whose countdown to retirement is now minus seven years.

But to Ken, fifty-five, retirement is a two-edged sword.

"I'm really looking forward to not having to work anymore and to do what I want, but at the same time, I'll be older than I am now," he says, smiling ruefully.

Ken admits that he's in reasonably good shape, but his poor middle-aged body is already starting to feel the effects of bursitis, arthritis, and more. "Within three months of turning forty, everything just started going," he recalls.

And after a weekend of home improvement projects now, "everything aches. I just don't spring up like I used to," Ken says.

Jill Vanderbrug, my former sixth-grade teacher, now fiftysomething and ready to retire in just a few more years, agrees.

"I have never heard so many people groaning and seen so many people walking funny," she reports. "Many of my colleagues seem to be moving a lot slower and complaining more about aching body parts. The longer you've been sitting, the harder it seems to get up and get moving with any conviction. Heaven help us if you have to chase someone for some reason!

"Maybe more vigorous exercise would help keep those muscles toned," she muses, ". . . in our spare time."

She needs a little Ben-Gay . . . and some vitamins.

Just before my cousin Susie turned fifty, her husband Chuck brought her home a bottle of Centrum Silver intended for the "senior set."

"I indignantly told him, in no uncertain terms, that maybe *he* was old enough for those, but I certainly never would be," she declared. "Guess what I take now every morning?"

Pat and Ken take a whole slew of vitamins—ranging from A to Zinc.

When they get together with friends their age, they find themselves comparing vitamins. "Are you taking E? What about C? You need to make sure you get some D."

Once they run out of vitamins, they turn their conversation to retirement and grandkids.

Pat and Ken can't join in the grandchildren chatter yet, but they are able to talk about their myriad granddogs and cats.

Judi says she and her husband Jim's conversations these days compared to ten or twenty years ago are much quieter.

"That's not to say we don't communicate," she says. "Sometimes we say volumes without uttering a word. Other times we finish each other's sentences, if not verbally, then mentally. Or what one of us forgets, the other (hopefully) remembers.

"We depend more on each other to fill in the blanks," she says, smiling.

Jim's a minister, so for thirty-three years of Sundays, Judi's listened to him preach.

"We often joke that if he were to die in the pulpit, I could finish his sermons without missing a beat—complete with illustrations," she says, laughing.

Bev Stroebel asked her seventy-year-old husband Bill if he thinks they talk to each other differently now in this stage of their lives compared to past years.

"I can't remember *how* we used to talk to each other," he replied.

But Bill certainly hasn't forgotten how to be romantic.

"About a year ago when I asked him how he could stand looking at my saggy body parts," Bev recalled, "he said, 'I still see a twenty-two-year-old—the age I was in 1954 when we married—when I look at you.'"

Now there's a man who knows how to give a compliment.

Not everyone is quite as skilled.

Or maybe, just maybe, those of us on the receiving end are just a tad bit touchy (and less gracious) these days.

For instance, one woman I know really well—who shall remain nameless—bit the head off her poor husband just because he said, "Honey, you look really nice today."

"What's that supposed to mean?" she snapped. "Do you mean I didn't look good *yesterday*?"

Another menopausal friend of mine blew up at someone for calling her "ma'am."

"I snapped at a girl in Starbucks," Karen recalled. "I told her, "Don't ever say 'ma'am' to any woman who walks through that door. We don't like it! If you don't know what we are, say 'miss.' If the woman's married, she'll let you know it's Mrs. If not, we'll just like being called 'miss',"she ended, with a smile.

I'm not sure just when I became a ma'am.

Remember that delightful TV show, *The Wonder Years*?

Well, I feel as if I've entered the invisible years.

When I was young and stationed overseas in the Air Force, I was used to getting attention from men—young and old. This was quite a heady experience for a rather naïve, impressionable nineteen-year-old wallflower who hadn't dated much and never went to the prom.

Suddenly, men were asking me out left and right. My dance card was always full, and my theme song became:

"I feel pretty, oh so pretty . . ."

American women were at a premium on base.

Especially single ones.

When I first arrived in Germany, I was one of only about thirty unattached women on a base of a few thousand men.

You do the math.

Talk about testosterone.

It was unsettling, however, because as I'd walk to work, guys would whistle or smile flirtatiously and say, "Hi, Laura," as they passed.

These were men I'd never met! How did they know my name?

I later learned that whenever orders arrived on base announcing the impending assignment of a new female, the word—and her name—spread like wildfire.

Actually, I think the actual terminology the guys used was a little less polite: "Fresh meat!"

After a while, you start to feel like that.

I'll never forget the morning I walked into the base coffee shop on my way to work to grab a doughnut and a quick cup of tea. I was in my dress blues: blouse, jacket, skirt—regulation length, just skimming my knees—nylons and pumps.

I pushed open the door and immediately saw that the place was packed—with men. There was nary a woman in sight.

I hesitated. For some reason, it suddenly felt overwhelming to be the lone woman in the middle of a hundred men. I felt vulnerable.

But then I thought, *Don't be silly, Laura! These are your fellow soldiers just drinking coffee and having breakfast before they go to work—just like you.*

So I walked through the door and headed for the order counter.

All chatter stopped as every male head swiveled my way.

Each shiny-pump-shod step I made past that raging sea of testosterone to the front of the room was frightening. I felt as if I was about to be devoured by a pack of hungry wolves.

I changed my order to go.

Now I still had to make my way back through the room.

"Hey, baby, lookin' good!"

"M'mmmm, nice legs."

"I want me some of that."

Once I made it safely out the door, I was shaking so badly, I spilled my tea.

I certainly didn't feel invisible that day—or during most of my Air Force years.

If anything, I felt too visible—too much on display— too much of an object, which wound up giving me a rather skewed and distorted perspective on men and my relationship to them for years afterward.

Therapy helped.

But these days—after twentysome years and thirtysome pounds—the only attention I garner is from the bag boy at the grocery store.

"Paper or plastic, ma'am?"

At first, this sudden invisibility factor was a little difficult to get used to.

It was as if I didn't even exist anymore.

And I know I'm not alone.

"It gets worse with every year," one woman said.

"It gets worse with every ten pounds," another added.

Yikes! No wonder my self-esteem was sagging—I had both the years *and* the pounds.

But my sister-in-law Sheri had a whole different take on the ma'am and invisibility thing.

"Young men treat you with respect now because they're not hitting on you," she said. "And I take full advantage of it . . . letting them help me out with my groceries and whatever else."

There's definitely something to be said for being able to relax now in a roomful of men and not worry about the whole predator thing.

It's called freedom.

My friend Ruth has had her "freedom" for several years now.

But she said one of the most difficult things that ever happened to her was turning fifty with no significant—or even insignificant—other in her life.

"I was also struggling to change careers without going in the poorhouse," she recalled. "So imagine my horror when I found a nice thick invitation in my mailbox from AARP (American Association of Retired Persons)."

After bringing it inside, Ruth shrieked and threw the envelope across the room.

"Not only did they know I had turned fifty, they were trying to take advantage of my vulnerability and get me to embrace senior citizenship," she said, indignantly.

"Over my dead body."

Some of us can get pretty hung up on our bodies—thinking flat stomachs, slender legs, and unlined faces define us.

A couple years ago, my mom was sorting through a box of pictures and came across one of me taken in high school—in the only formal I ever wore during my teenage years—for the local Junior Miss pageant.

Yep. I was in a beauty pageant.

Me—the girl who never got asked to a prom or homecoming.

The girl whose Dad-hero had died when she was just fifteen.

The editor of the school paper who at seventeen loudly spouted popular '70s feminist rhetoric as self-defense for never being asked out.

The same girl who never felt pretty all through high school.

Being in a beauty pageant gave me that affirmation I craved as a seventeen-year-old, although of course I told everyone I was doing it for the prize money. (Which I didn't win, by the way.)

Mom brought the picture over to our house, thinking Michael might want to see it.

"Gee, honey, bet you wish you knew me then, huh?" I said flirtatiously as Michael looked at my thirty-pound thinner, still-double-breasted self.

"No," he said, gently caressing my cheek. "I think you're much prettier now."

I don't have to worry about Michael ever finding me invisible.

Back off, ladies, he's mine.

After a certain number of years, our faces become our biographies.

CYNTHIA OZICK

eighteen

Mother Said There'd Be Days like This

She just never told me
they'd last for months.

Age is not all decay; it is the ripening, the swelling, of the fresh life within, that withers and bursts the husk.

GEORGE MACDONALD

My best friend says I've gotten "hipper" as I've gotten older.

Or was it hippier?

One thing I have gotten is less logical.

Case in point: Michael decided one day that he was going to replace our loud, annoying doorbell—that always made Gracie and me jump in fright—with one that had more dulcet tones.

Early one Saturday morning he went to the local hardware store, returning shortly thereafter with a doorbell that had pretty chimes instead. "Now all I have to do is find the transformer and I can hook it up for you," he said, kissing me on the cheek, eager to get to work. "Honey, I don't suppose you've seen it, have you?" he asked hopefully.

"What?"

"The transformer for the doorbell."

"No, sorry," I said, regretfully.

"Well, it shouldn't be too hard to find," he said cheerfully. "It's probably out in the garage or in one of the closets."

Several hours later, after cleaning out a few closets *and* the kitchen pantry, Michael was a little less cheerful. (He'd had to pull everything out to try to find the transformer, so decided he might as well organize things a bit before putting them back in.)

A couple more exhausting hours later, he sought me out and said, "Well, I finally found it."

"Oh, good, honey. Where?"

"In the garage," he said, leading me past the washer and dryer to point up to a tiny, little black box high on one garage wall, partially obscured by the water heater.

"Oh, is *that* what you were looking for?" I said cluelessly. "I knew that was there."

"Why didn't you TELL me?" Michael roared in not-so-dulcet tones.

"You said you were looking for a TRANSFORMER," I said with an injured air. "I didn't know that was a *transformer*. I just knew it was the doorbell thingy."

Even though the doorbell didn't get installed that day, it wasn't a total loss.

The closets were more organized than they'd been in months.

Case Two: Recently, while proofreading a letter Michael had written, I looked up a word in the American Heritage Dictionary to be sure of its exact meaning. We bantered back and forth for a while about some other "L" words until an entry at the top of the page caught my honey's eye: *Loony: so as to appear demented.*

"H'mmmm," he said, marking the spot.

A few minutes later, something in the letter reminded me of an old familiar folk song, so of course I immediately began singing.

Michael, my trained-singer husband, had never heard the song before.

I couldn't believe he didn't know it.

"It's a classic," I said incredulously. "We sang it in grade school; *every*body knows it! In fact, it's probably in the big green songbook we inherited from my stepfather."

"The big green songbook was from my grandmother," Michael replied.

"No, it was Mort's," I insisted. "It was in the old piano bench."

Suddenly, a horrible thought struck me. "Oh no," I said. "Did you give the book away with the piano when you got rid of it?"

"Dear, I was out of town when *you* gave away the piano. Remember?" Michael said patiently. "When I came home, it was gone."

"Oh, that's right," I said a little sheepishly.

Michael picked up the dictionary, handed it to me, and pointed to the "L" word on the page he'd marked.

I think loony runs in my family. Take my cousin Susie for example.

"Never noticing that the garage door did not go up all the way, I proceeded to drive right through it," said Susie, who lives in Colorado. "It wasn't until boards lay splintered and the spring came crashing down that I realized something was amiss.

"We did get a new improved garage door out of the episode," she added, "which helped to appease my husband."

Appeasing husbands is an important thing.

Unfortunately, Susie's looniness didn't end there.

"All in one day, I placed the ice cream in the cupboard and my coffee cup in the freezer," she said. "The next morning, I found syrupy goo dripping from the cupboard onto the counter and a very blue mug—I was sure it had been pink the day before—in severe hypothermia."

Hormones are the culprit.

"It used to be so simple," said Judi. "Life for a woman was divided into four parts: childhood, childbearing, childfree, childish.

"Then you died.

161

"Now there's PMS, perimenopause, menopause, post-menopause . . . and no one seems to be able to tell me how to know when you finish one and start the next," she said.

"It's like staying in school forever with no hope of graduating.

"I think at this point I've moved up from PMS, passed peri, and done a semester of menopause," Judi said. "I'm just hoping to get my diploma while I still have a brain left to use it."

There's one thing most of us wish we *didn't* have left. Periods.

"Just when you think you're done at last, a renegade comes from out of nowhere," said Jill. "I went ten months with nothing, then got one that lasted eighteen days."

She's not the only one who's been dealt an unexpected menstrual cycle.

I know women who could see her eighteen days and raise her three more.

Say hello to yours truly.

For the past nine years since I've finished chemo-therapy I never know when that renegade's going to return for a visit—or how long he'll stay.

My new friend Diana says she's been "forced into meno-pause" because when she was diagnosed with breast can-cer, she wasn't menopausal, she was still doing her monthly thing.

But after her second chemotherapy treatment, she's never had another period.

"I was always miserable with that anyway," Diana said, "so my husband wanted to know which I'd prefer; men-struating every month or having the hot flashes.

"I told him neither, but if I had to choose, I'd take the flashes; at least I don't have to buy any supplies for that."

Supplies or not, Karen would like to know what her big reward is for getting older and going through hot flashes.

"I had a hysterectomy, so it's not the periods," she said. "I got that reward right after surgery.

"Is the sagging my reward?"

Karen finally figured out that the reward is the discounts you get now when you go to Denny's.

Charlotte Adelsperger got an even better reward than that.

One sizzling July evening, she stepped into the batter's box, took a practice swing, and eyed the pitcher.

"Get a hit, Mom!" her thirty-year-old daughter Karen called from the bench.

"You can do it!" her granddaughter Melinda echoed.

Charlotte took the first pitch—a little outside. When the pitcher lobbed the ball with a high arch down the middle of the plate, she leveled her swing and smacked it over second base.

A solid hit to center.

"Myriad thoughts swept over me," Charlotte recalled. "Here I am in my sixties playing on a women's slow-pitch softball team and I'm old enough to be mother to any of them. But I just made it to first base! I'm glad I took the risk to play again—me, a breast cancer survivor—a victory lady."

Before the first game Charlotte checked out everything: "I cleaned my glasses, popped in removable dental bridges, and shoved my breast prosthesis into place," she recalled.

"During the seventh inning I was up to bat again. I knocked another single. My running felt like slow motion compared to the other players, but I made it to first."

After the game, someone came up to Charlotte and asked her, 'How'd you get all those hits?"

"Must be the help of my trifocals," she replied, laughing.

Charlotte's softball experience taught her how satisfying it can be to take the risk to get back in action—"even if you are the oldest one on the team."

My friend June, who is in her seventies, says that she has learned that life goes on no matter what happens to her.

"Life doesn't center around me," she says. "The sun rises in the morning and sets at night. The stars and moon appear and then fade at daylight—just like the Lord created them to do.

"Life goes on. And I've learned that I can go on also—in spite of or because of bad and/or sad situations."

After her husband's death, June discovered that she could continue to live.

"To live—not just exist," she says. "Once again, I hear the music of life. At age twenty, I was sure I could handle just about anything," she said, reflecting back. "After all, I was young and had lots of answers. Just ask me the questions.

"Now I tend to plod a bit, questioning whether or not I'm able to handle a situation. Oh yes, I have many questions in my senior years. And I intend to keep asking and seeking and keeping on."

Me too, June.

Like June, when I was twenty, I too had lots of answers.

Actually, I thought I had them all, and nobody could tell me any different. I charged through life doing whatever I wanted whenever I wanted.

Life was one big party.

But, truth is, I spent a lot of time chasing after I didn't know what.

Sure, I traveled to lots of fun and exciting places (London, Paris, Amsterdam, Munich, Athens), met interesting people, and did things I'd never done before: I skied in the Swiss Alps, rode in a gondola in Venice, and flew a glider over the English countryside.

But my twenties were also lonely, confusing times of fear, desperation, and deep longing.

Simply put, I was a mess.

So much so that at the age of twenty-seven, I was on the verge of suicide.

I already felt dead and used up, so why not make it official?

Then my friend Pat led me to Christ.

And I was given new life. "If anyone is in Christ, he is a new creation; the old has gone, the new has come!" (2 Cor. 5:17).

You couldn't pay me to go back to my twenties.

I love the life I have now.

I have a deep and abiding faith in my Lord and Savior Jesus Christ; I'm coming up on ten years of marriage to my soulmate Michael; I've been cancer-free for nearly nine years; we live in a cozy little house in a cozy little neighborhood with our sweet little dog, Gracie, and we have close friends and family who are precious to us.

Plus, I'm getting paid to do what I love most—write.

How can I complain?

If this is middle age, then bring it on!

But, Lord, could you please maybe hold off on that gravity thing a little longer?

Grow old along with me! The best is yet to be.
Robert Browning

nineteen

Don't Throw in the Towel

Use it to absorb those hot flash sweats.
(And other ways to take care of your over-forty self.)

It is never too late to be what you might have been.

GEORGE ELIOT

Okay, so you're "middle-aged."

You're over forty.

So what?

I hate to coin an old cliché, but life really *can* begin at forty.

It certainly did for me.

That was when my lifelong dream of becoming a published author came true. And it's been uphill ever since.

Well, except for a few body parts.

But who's counting?

So quit whining—I'm saying this to myself too, since I've been known to be a bit of a whiner *occasionally*—and just relax and learn to be comfortable in your middle-age skin, sagging as it may be.

If you're not sure how to go about that, here are a few helpful hints.

How to Take Care of Your Over-Forty Self

1. Draw a big bath filled with your favorite relaxing bath salts and drink a nice hot "cuppa" tea.
2. Treat yourself to a massage.
3. Join a gym—if you must.
4. Or do what those of us who HATE exercise do: walk instead.
5. Exfoliate.
6. Drink plenty of water.
7. Go to bed early.

8. Invest in flannel sheets.
9. Floss.
10. Read.
11. Snuggle with a beloved pet.
12. Say no to energy-wasting activities you really don't want to do.
13. Say yes to daffodils and drives in the country.
14. Plan to quit that soul-sucking job you hate and go for your dream job.
15. Always keep a large supply of sticky notes on hand.
16. Invest in a Velcro handle for your day planner that can attach to your belt or waistband. If there isn't one in stores yet, then invent it.
17. Moisturize.
18. Get a facial.
19. Rearrange the living room.
20. Stop listening to the "You should . . ." sayers who try to fit you into a narrow, little age-conforming box: "You should grow up and get a *real* job; very few people make it as a writer . . ."
    "You should cut your hair; older women look better with short hair."
21. Turn off the TV and listen to the silence.
22. Read the Psalms before going to sleep.
23. Eat pizza on the good china.
24. Rethink old attitudes and opinions. I was never, ever, a dog person: "Ugh; they bark, shed, make messes." And I certainly could *not* understand people who talked to their animals in baby-speak: "Awww . . . does Mommy's widdle pwecious want to go for a walkie around the blockie?" And now I can't imagine my life without Gracie—nor could

Michael. But I won't bore you anymore with the speshul widdle Gwacie-langwage we speak.

25. Don't use your age as an excuse for not doing things.
26. Eat chocolate.
27. Take your vitamins.
28. Treat yourself to a pedicure.
29. Challenge your comfort zone—try something you've never done before but always secretly yearned to do: skydiving, mountain climbing, tap-dancing. If that's a little too adventurous for you, then start with something smaller—try out a new color you never thought you could wear—for me, it was beige.
30. Listen.
31. Go to a matinee and eat popcorn—with butter.
32. Renew your library card.
33. Do something nice for a stranger.
34. Practice generosity.
35. Call your mom.
36. Read a story to a child.
37. Clean out your junk drawer.
38. Get rid of any clothes that make you look fat.
39. Volunteer at a school, nursing home, or homeless shelter.
40. Start the day with God.
41. Eat breakfast.
42. Walk the dog.
43. Call an old friend.
44. Make a new friend.
45. Keep a steady supply of Tums on hand.
46. Get your yearly mammogram! Don't put it off—trust me on this.

47. Buy that expensive perfume you've always wanted.
48. Look up at the stars.
49. Expect less, accept more. Stop setting unrealistic expectations of your friends and family and instead, learn to accept graciously what they're able to offer.
50. Dance with abandon.
51. Write an old-fashioned letter on nice stationery—not typewritten or e-mailed—to someone near and dear to you who lives far away.
52. Send a pretty card to a good friend who lives in the same town (buy one that's blank inside so you can pen your own thoughts).
53. Go on a contemplative retreat and enjoy the solitude.
54. Pray.
55. Rejoice in the Lord's creation.
56. Go fishing—unless like me, you can't stand putting the worm on the hook. In that case, rent *A River Runs Through It* instead or just watch a rerun of Andy and Opie fishing.
57. Sing more.
58. Don't stifle your laughter—let loose with that belly laugh when you feel the need.
59. Try the Thighmaster (or if you can't afford it, just follow along with the commercial and afterwards curl up with a good book instead).
60. Remember that God made you and loves you: wrinkles, puffy thighs, and all.

And if none of this quite does it, you can always just . . .
    Deny.
    Deny.
    Deny.

Do not conform any longer to the pattern of this world, but be transformed by the renewing of your mind.

ROMANS 12:2A

For information about speaking engagements, retreats, luncheons, or one-day events, please contact Laura Jensen Walker c/o Revell Publicity (or e-mail Laura at Ljenwalk@aol.com).